S

D0450879

Best Easy Day Hikes
Lake Tahoe

Help Us Keep This Guide Up to Date

Every effort has been made by the author and editors to make this guide as accurate and useful as possible. However, many things can change after a guide is published—trails are rerouted, regulations change, facilities come under new management, and so forth.

We appreciate hearing from you concerning your experiences with this guide and how you feel it could be improved and kept up to date. While we may not be able to respond to all comments and suggestions, we'll take them to heart, and we'll also make certain to share them with the author. Please send your comments and suggestions to the following address:

Globe Pequot Press
Reader Response/Editorial Department
246 Goose Lane
Guilford, CT 06437

Or you may e-mail us at:

editorial@falcon.com

Thanks for your input, and happy trails!

Best Easy Day Hikes Series

Best Easy Day Hikes
Lake Tahoe

Third Edition

Tracy Salcedo-Chourré

FALCONGUIDES

GUILFORD, CONNECTICUT
HELENA, MONTANA

S

FALCONGUIDES®

An imprint of Rowman & Littlefield
Falcon, FalconGuides, and Outfit Your Mind are registered trademarks
of Rowman & Littlefield.

Distributed by NATIONAL BOOK NETWORK

Copyright © 2015 by Rowman & Littlefield

Maps: Off Route Inc. © Rowman & Littlefield
TOPO! Explorer software and SuperQuad source maps courtesy of
National Geographic Maps. For information about TOPO! Explorer,
TOPO!, and Nat Geo Maps products, go to www.topo.com or www.
natgeomaps.com.

British Library Cataloguing-in-Publication Information Available

Library of Congress Cataloging-in-Publication Data Available

ISBN 978-0-7627-9687-8 (alk. paper)
ISBN 978-1-4930-1430-9 (e-book)

♾™ The paper used in this publication meets the minimum require-
ments of American National Standard for Information Sciences—
Permanence of Paper for Printed Library Materials, ANSI/NISO
Z39.48-1992.

To the Friedman and Rodman families

Contents

The Hikes

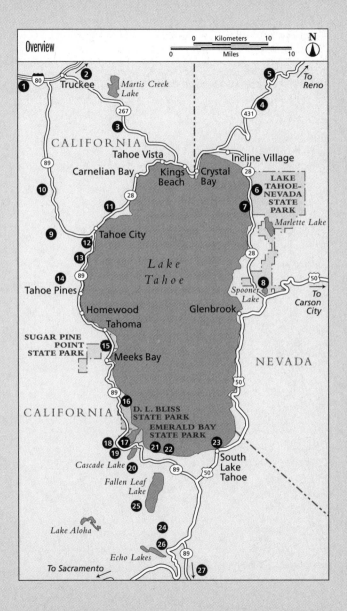

Acknowledgments

Thanks to the following folks for their advice and help with the first edition of this guide: Mike St. Michel and Don Lane of the US Forest Service Lake Tahoe Basin Management Unit; Dave Nettle of Alpenglow Sports; Gisela Steiner of Tahoe Trail Trekkers; Bill Schneider; and editors David Lee, Charlene Patterson, and Erica Olsen.

Thanks to these folks for help and review of the second edition: Don Lane and Lindsay Gusses of the Lake Tahoe Basin Management Unit; Mark Kimbrough, executive director of the Tahoe Rim Trail Association; Hal Paris and Pandora Bahlman of the Incline Village General Improvement District; Roger Adamson, park superintendent of the Tahoe City Public Utility District; Bill Houdyschell of the forestry division of the Tahoe Donner Association; Bill Champion of Lake Tahoe–Nevada State Park; Dean Lutz, Jeff Wiley, and Susanne Jensen of Tahoe National Forest; and Jacqui Zink, park ranger with the US Army Corps of Engineers at Martis Creek Lake.

Thanks to these folks for their help with the third edition: Morgan Fessler of the Tahoe Rim Trail Association; Scott Elliott of the California State Parks, Sierra State Parks Foundation; Garrett Villanueva of the Lake Tahoe Basin Management Unit; Jacqui Zink of the US Army Corps of Engineers.

Thanks to these folks for everything: Julie Roth and Oliver Aslin, the Friedman/Rodman clan; the Salcedo clan; the Chourré clan; and my sons, Cruz, Jesse, and Penn.

Introduction

You'd think, pulling together a third edition of this guide to the best easy day hikes around Lake Tahoe, that I'd have figured out exactly how to capture in words the magic of the Sierra Nevada's most amazing "glacial gem."

But I haven't.

Perhaps that's because the place feels like home. From shoreline to rim, whether tramping through the fragrant woods or diving off the back of a boat into the bottomless blue, Tahoe is familiar and welcoming. Adventurer, wanderer, seeker, romantic, student, environmentalist, lazy slug who wants no more than a warm slab of granite on which to recline . . . Tahoe satisfies every aspect of my being.

I'm not special in this way. Any hiker venturing onto any trail on a blue-sky summer day is bound to feel profound contentment in the embrace of the lake and basin.

The 27 easy day hikes described in this edition include favorites that will never lose their appeal, a handful of lovely additions, and brief reprises of trails that didn't make the cut for lack of space. The routes are intended to showcase the various facets of Lake Tahoe and its environs, from lakeside to ridgeline, forest to meadow, and historic site to solitude.

Even when it's not visible, the lake informs each trail. Selecting the "best" day hikes continues to present a pleasant conundrum—the options are numerous, and there's not a dud in the bunch. The trick has been to pick hikes that will satisfy intrepid visitor and curious resident alike: to include something for everyone. Thus these hikes range from super-short wheelchair-accessible interpretive trails to thigh-burning treks to high-altitude viewpoints. Some routes are ideal for adventure, some for contemplation. Others are perfect for a Sunday afternoon outing with the family, and yet others for winding down on a summer evening after a hard day's work.

My hope is that you'll be inspired to hike farther and more often. Onward and upward.

Tahoe in Brief

People have been drawn to the Lake Tahoe basin for thousands of years. The Washoe traveled up from the lowlands that now cradle Reno to fish, hunt, and harvest summer's woodland bounty. With the discovery of gold and silver in the mid-1800s, trails that had once been passable only in summer became year-round routes traveled by forty-niners and the entrepreneurs—shopkeepers, tavern owners, bakers, cattlemen—who followed them. Miners' cabins, flumes, and other remnants of California's gold rush and Nevada's Comstock Lode can be found along some of these routes.

Once the booms went bust, the wildland lovers moved in—renowned wilderness advocates such as John Muir and others—and the trails became paths enjoyed by vacationers. Resorts sprang up around the lake, enabling visitors in the early twentieth century to explore the backcountry and then retire to lakeside estates with superlative views. Trails lead to several of these resorts, the most spectacular being Vikingsholm at the head of Emerald Bay.

These days, folks gather in winter and summer alike to enjoy holidays by the lake, while others call the blue heart of the Sierra home. Invariably they end up outside, lured by the dramatic landscape into the fresh pine-scented air. Invariably they want to take a hike.

The Nature of Tahoe

Tahoe's trails range from rugged and mountainous to flat and paved. Hikes in this guide cover the gamut. While by definition a Best Easy Day Hike poses little danger to the traveler, knowing a few details about the nature of the Lake Tahoe region will enhance your explorations.

Lake Tahoe, at 6,224 feet, sits square in the montane zone. Lower down in this zone, the forests are dominated by Jeffrey pines and fragrant ponderosa pines, and pocked with meadows that blossom in early summer. Higher up, lodgepole pine and red fir flourish. Most of the routes in this guide are in the montane zone, but a few brush the ecotone with the subalpine zone, where the whitebark pines and mountain hemlocks may be stunted by winter snows. The subalpine zone begins near 9,000 feet and reaches to treeline.

Take altitude into consideration when hiking at Lake Tahoe, particularly if you come from sea level. Altitude sickness is a possibility. If you or a member of your hiking party experiences any symptoms of this illness, including headache, nausea, or unusual fatigue, descend to a lower altitude immediately and seek medical attention.

The hiking season around Lake Tahoe generally stretches from the first of May to the end of October, with trails at lower elevations melting off before those at higher elevations. The opening of any particular trail is dependent on the amount of winter snowfall and the speed of the snowmelt. Snowshoe hikers and cross-country skiers can travel into areas traversed by these trails during winter, weather and backcountry skills permitting.

Afternoon thunderstorms are fairly common in the summer months and taper off by autumn. Regardless of the season, hikers should be prepared for changeable weather—rain, cold, snow, or heat—by wearing layers and packing waterproof gear.

Black bears are commonly seen around Lake Tahoe. If you encounter a bear on the trail, do not run. Stand still and make noise, and the bear will most likely scram. Never come between a mama bear and her cubs—if you see cubs, leave the area immediately.

Support Tahoe-Truckee Trails

To learn more about trails and parklands around Lake Tahoe and neighboring communities, or to support trail building and maintenance, contact any one of the organizations listed below.

- Tahoe Rim Trail Association: (775) 298-4485; tahoe rimtrail.org
- Sierra State Parks Foundation: (530) 583-9911; sierra stateparks.org
- Truckee Trails Foundation: truckeetrails.org

How to Use This Guide

Each hike is described with a map and summary information that delivers the trail's vital statistics including length, difficulty, fees and permits, park hours, canine compatibility, and trail contacts.

Directions to the trailhead are provided, including the GPS coordinates of the trailhead. Starting points for driving directions are the largest communities on the lakeshore: Incline Village on the North Shore, Tahoe City on the West Shore, and South Lake Tahoe/Stateline on the South Shore. A scenic highway, variously designated CA 89, CA 28, NV 28, and US 50, circumnavigates the lake; directions to trailheads are given from this road. Directions for trails in Donner and Truckee are given from I-80.

Information about what you'll see along the trail, as well as tidbits about natural and cultural history, is provided in the narrative hike description. A detailed route finder (Miles and Directions) sets forth mileages between significant landmarks along the trail.

How the Hikes Were Chosen

Hikes in this guide range in difficulty from flat excursions perfect for family outings to more challenging treks to highland lakes. In addition to trails that begin in the lake basin itself, a few are in surrounding communities like Truckee and Tahoe Donner. Wherever your starting point, I've suggested an easy day hike nearby.

While these trails are among the best, keep in mind that other trails in the same area may be better suited to your needs. Potential alternatives are suggested in the Options sections at the ends of hike descriptions.

To freshen up the third edition, some hikes that appeared in previous editions of this guide were bumped to make room for new alternatives. These excluded routes, along with summary information about how to reach them, are listed in the Options section of the nearest hike.

Selecting a Hike

These are all easy hikes, but "easy" is a relative term. Some would argue that no hike involving any kind of climbing is easy, but around Lake Tahoe climbs are a fact of life. Keep in mind that what you think is easy is entirely dependent on your level of fitness and the adequacy of your gear (primarily shoes). Use the trail's length as a gauge of its relative difficulty—even if climbing is involved, it won't be bad if the hike is less than 1 mile long. In addition to listing hikes that might appeal to the hiker seeking a certain experience, the Trail Finder lists the trails by level of difficulty. If you are hiking with a group, select a hike that's appropriate for the least fit/least prepared in your party.

Approximate hiking times are based on the assumption that on flat ground, most walkers average 2 miles per hour. Adjust that rate by the steepness of the terrain and your level of fitness (subtract time if you're an aerobic animal and add time if you're hiking with kids), and you have a ballpark hiking duration. Be sure to add more time if you plan to picnic or take part in other activities like birding or photography.

Trail Finder

Best Hikes for Lake Lovers
Skunk Harbor
Spooner Lake Loop
Vikingsholm and Emerald Point
Pacific Crest Trail at Echo Lakes
Five Lakes Trail

Best Hikes for River/Stream Lovers
Martis Creek Wildlife Area
Sagehen Creek
Truckee River Trail

Best Hikes for Waterfalls
Galena Falls
Cascade Falls
Shirley Canyon Cascades

Best Hikes for Meadow Lovers
Tahoe Meadows Interpretive Loop
Page Meadows
Antone Meadows
Big Meadow

Best Hikes for Children
Sand Harbor Nature Trail
Rainbow Trail
Angora Lakes

Best Hikes for History Lovers
The Lighthouse and Rubicon Point
Vikingsholm and Emerald Point
Lake of the Sky Trail and Tallac Historic Site
Glen Alpine

Best Hikes for a Workout
Ellis Peak Trail
General Creek Loop
Five Lakes Trail

Trails by Difficulty (Easiest to Hardest)
Sand Harbor Nature Trail
Rainbow Trail
Angora Lakes
Tahoe Meadows Interpretive Loop
Spooner Lake Loop
Lam Watah Trail
Sagehen Creek
Shirley Canyon Cascades
Lakeside Interpretive Trail at Donner Lake
Skunk Harbor
Eagle Lake
Lake of the Sky Trail and Tallac Historic Site
Truckee River Trail
Page Meadows
Big Meadow
Pacific Crest Trail at Echo Lakes
Martis Creek Wildlife Area
Glen Alpine
General Creek Loop
Antone Meadows
Galena Falls
Cascade Falls
Vikingsholm and Emerald Point
The Lighthouse and Rubicon Point
Cathedral Lake
Five Lakes Trail
Ellis Peak Trail

Map Legend

	Interstate Highway
	US Highway
	State Highway
	Local Road
	Unpaved Road
	Featured Trail
	Trail
	Boardwalk
	State Line
	River/Creek
	Body of Water
	Marsh/Swamp
	State Park/Wilderness Area
	Bench
	Boat Launch
	Bridge
	Camping
	Gate
	Information Center
	Lighthouse
	Parking
	Peak
	Picnic Area
	Point of Interest/Structure
	Restroom
	Town
	Trailhead
	Viewpoint/Overlook
	Waterfall

1 Lakeside Interpretive Trail at Donner Lake

Lake Tahoe gets all the glory, but this satellite lake, also deep and blue, is traced by an interpretive trail that shines a spotlight on both the spectacular setting and the remarkable, disturbing history of the infamous Donner Pass.

Start: Parking lot for the picnic area near the gauging station. You can also start at the park visitor center.

Distance: 2.4 miles out and back

Hiking time: About 2 hours

Difficulty: Easy

Trail surface: Dirt singletrack, barrier-free

Best seasons: Spring, summer, fall

Other trail users: None

Trail amenities: Restrooms, picnic facilities, camping

Canine compatibility: Leashed dogs permitted in developed picnic areas, but not China Cove

Fees and permits: Day-use fee to enter the park. Free parking is available along Donner Pass Road outside the park. To reach the trailhead from outside the park, follow the park road to the visitor center.

Schedule: Visitor center (museum) hours are from 10 a.m. to 5 p.m. daily

Maps: USGS Truckee and Norden CA; park trail map available at the entrance station and on an information board at the entrance

Trail contact: Donner Memorial State Park, 12593 Donner Pass Rd., Truckee, CA 96161; (530) 582-7892; www.parks.ca.gov. Sierra State Parks Foundation (info about Tahoe-Truckee area state parks), sierrastateparks.org.

Other: While at the park you can visit the Emigrant Trail Museum (open 10 a.m. to 5 p.m. daily); the Pioneer Monument; and the Murphy family cabin site (a remnant of the Donner expedition). Contact ReserveAmerica (800-444-7275; reserveamerica.com) for camping reservations.

Finding the trailhead: Take CA 89 from Tahoe City or CA 28 from Kings Beach to I-80 in Truckee. Head west on I-80 to the Donner Pass Road exit (about 0.7 mile west of the CA 89 interchange with I-80). Go left (south) on Donner Pass Road to the well-signed park entrance on the left (south). The trailhead is in the parking lot for the picnic area. Follow the park road past the entrance station and across the bridge, staying right at the gated campground road. The signed lot is on the right. GPS: N39 19.415' / W120 14.220'

The Hike

The story of the Donner Party is one of the grimmest in the history of the American West. Trapped by deep snow below the summit of what would become known as Donner Pass in the winter of 1846–47, these embattled emigrants—they'd already encountered a number of hardships on their cross-country passage—endured madness, despair, and cannibalism in their fight to survive. More than thirty souls perished in the scattering of cabins and camps the travelers established around Donner Lake; two of those cabin sites are preserved within the park boundaries.

No worries of such trauma on this hike, however—it's barely long or arduous enough to warrant a pause for a handful of trail mix. The route also sheds light on how this rugged high country was eventually rendered habitable, with interpretive panels describing settlement and industry in the area and the construction of the railroad and highway that would eventually make travel over the infamous pass relatively easy, even in winter.

The interpretive part of the trail is located at its west end; if you pay the entrance fee, you can park at the beach at China Cove and hike back toward the entrance station.

It's described here beginning at the picnic area at the Donner Creek dam. You can also start at the parks visitor center.

The trail begins at a small sign near the gauging station on Donner Creek, with the blue-green lake welling up alongside the dirt track. It roughly parallels the park road, with access to lakeside beaches, picnic grounds, and restrooms along most of its length. Expect some road noise from the nearby interstate and the park road—and the occasional rumble and whistle blow of a train riding high on the mountainside to the south—but you'll also be able to hear birds chirping in the lakeside brambles and the wind whirring through the treetops.

Tile mosaics touting the benefits of recycling, healthy forests, and responsible development, created by local fifth-graders, line the trailside at the 0.3-mile mark. The open forest allows glimpses of the gray granite heights of Donner Peak and Schallenberger Ridge to the south and west. A chain of picnic areas begins with a prime spot on a spit of sand on the southeast shore of the lake, with views across the water to lakeshore cabins on the north side.

The interpretive signs begin here too, focusing on the human and natural history of the area and touching on the role fire plays in the maintenance of forest health, the geologic origins of the Sierra Nevada, the Native Americans that summered in the area, early European settlement, construction of a wagon road over the pass in the 1850s, and completion of the interstate in the 1960s.

China Cove's crescent beach, with great views across the lake to the western peaks and ridges, is at trail's end. Picnic tables and restrooms make this the perfect place for lunch and relaxing. Return as you came (the most scenic route), or follow the park road back to the trailhead.

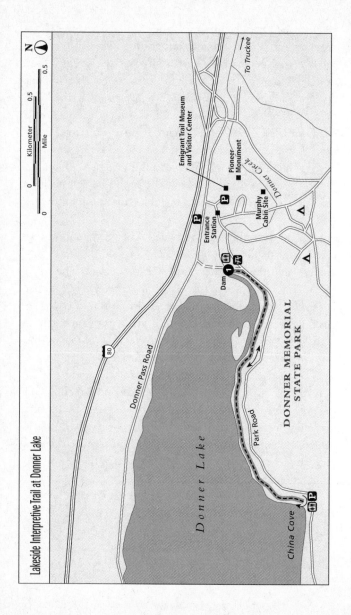

Lakeside Interpretive Trail at Donner Lake

Donner Lake

80

Donner Pass Road

China Cove

Park Road

DONNER MEMORIAL
STATE PARK

Dam

Entrance
Station

P

P

Emigrant Trail Museum
and Visitor Center

Pioneer
Monument

Murphy
Cabin Site

Donner Creek

To Truckee

N

Kilometer
0   0.5

Mile
0   0.5

Miles and Directions

0.0   Start in the picnic area parking lot at the trail sign near the gauging station. Head southwest on the obvious waterside path.

0.3   Pass the tile mosaics.

0.5   Pass a picnic site on a sand spit, then more picnic sites on the left (south) side of the trail.

1.2   Reach the beach at China Cove. Take a break and read the last of the interpretive signs, then retrace your steps to the trailhead.

2.4   Arrive back at the trailhead.

2 Sagehen Creek

A lovely trail leads through wildflower-filled meadows and woodlands to the shoreline of an arm of Stampede Reservoir.

Start: Unsigned trailhead alongside CA 89 north of Truckee
Distance: 4.7 miles out and back
Hiking time: 2–3 hours
Difficulty: Easy
Trail surface: Dirt singletrack
Best seasons: Late spring, summer, fall
Other trail users: Mountain bikers, trail runners
Trail amenities: Parking for about 15 cars in a roadside pullout
Canine compatibility: Leashed dogs permitted

Fees and permits: None
Schedule: Sunrise–sunset daily
Maps: USGS Hobart Mills CA
Trail contact: Tahoe National Forest, Truckee Ranger District, 10811 Stockrest Springs Rd., Truckee, CA 96161; (530) 587-3558; www.fs.usda.gov/tahoe
Special considerations: The meadowlands and creek foster a healthy population of insects in spring. To enjoy the wildflower display without losing pints of blood, use bug juice and dress appropriately.

Finding the trailhead: From the junction of CA 267/CA 89 and I-80 in Truckee, head north on CA 89 toward Sierraville and Graeagle. The unsigned parking area for the trailhead is 7.3 miles north of the junction with the interstate, at the bottom of a substantial hill and on the right side of the roadway. GPS: N39 26.040' / W120 12.297'

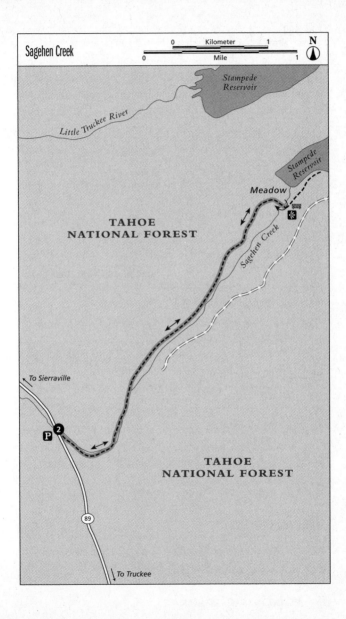

Kilometer

Mile

N

Stampede
Reservoir

Little Truckee River

Stampede
Reservoir

Meadow

**TAHOE
NATIONAL FOREST**

Sagehen Creek

To Sierraville

P **2**

**TAHOE
NATIONAL FOREST**

89

To Truckee

The Hike

This gentle ramble leads through meadowlands alongside Sagehen Creek to a remote arm of the Stampede Reservoir. The trail is flat and straightforward, with plenty of wildflowers in season and wonderful views across the reservoir year-round.

Begin by rambling along the creek side, avoiding the side paths leading to the right, down to the stream. Willows and small aspen crowd the path. Bend to the northeast and the creek drainage widens, skunk cabbage growing amid grasses in the gentle valley.

At about the 1-mile mark, as the trail traverses above Sagehen Creek, you can look down to the right onto a shallow pond, which may be dry in late season or under drought conditions. Young pines have begun to colonize the grasslands, though the evergreens grow relatively thick on the steeper slope to the left.

The path widens into a doubletrack as it heads across a broadening meadow, with views of Stampede Reservoir ahead. Pass through the wildflowers and into parklike stands of evergreens. Timbers form a bridge over a side stream. Continue through the grasses to a second bridge, this one constructed of planks, which spans the main channel of Sagehen Creek.

The turnaround point is a bench that offers great views of the quiet waters of Stampede Reservoir. An overgrown trail continues south through the marshy grasslands, which you can explore if you desire. Otherwise, return as you came.

Miles and Directions

0.0   Start by heading down the trail alongside Sagehen Creek.

1.0   Pass a small, shallow pond.

1.7 The trail separates into a doubletrack and enters a broad meadow.

2.3 Cross a bridge made of hewn timber.

2.4 Cross the main channel of Sagehen Creek. Enjoy views of Stampede Reservoir from a bench, then return as you came.

4.8 Arrive back at the trailhead.

Options: The Northwoods Interpretive Nature Trail, a second-edition favorite that also lies just outside Truckee, explores the meadows and woodlands surrounding Trout Creek within the Tahoe Donner subdivision. No worries if you don't have a field guide: Interpretive signs along the track describe bears and birds of prey, wildflowers and willows, trout and trees. The boardwalk section is particularly inviting, with wildflowers flourishing in late spring and summer. The 2.1-mile loop, which takes about an hour to complete, is composed of singletrack and boardwalks and is easy to follow, with white blazes on trees also marking the route. The trail is suitable for children and can be traversed from late spring through fall (watch for bugs in early season). Leashed dogs are permitted.

To reach the trailhead from downtown Truckee, head west on I-80 to the Donner Pass Road exit (about 0.7 mile west of the CA 89 interchange). Go right (east) on Donner Pass Road for 0.4 mile to Northwoods Boulevard. Turn left (north) onto Northwoods Boulevard and go 1.4 miles to the Northwoods Clubhouse and parking lot on the right (east). The signed trailhead is in the northwest corner of the clubhouse parking lot. GPS: N39 20.624' / W120 12.991'

Beyond the Northwoods trail, an expanding network of multiuse trails offers a variety of opportunities for exploration throughout Tahoe Donner. Many follow fire roads and offer great views of Donner Lake and the Truckee River valley. For details about access, download a trail map at tahoe donner.com/wordpress/wp-content/uploads/2012/03/TrailMap_Summer2013_7.16.2013.pdf. For more information, contact the Tahoe Donner Association Member Services Office, 11509 Northwoods Blvd., Truckee, CA 96161; (530) 587-9400; tahoedonner.com.

For more information on Truckee area trails, visit the Truckee Trails Foundation at truckeetrails.org. The Truckee Donner Chamber of Commerce also maintains an online database of information about the mountain town, including where to eat, where to stay, and local events. Visit the site at truckee.com, or contact the chamber by calling (530) 587-8808.

3 Martis Creek Wildlife Area

Wildlife abounds around Martis Creek, thriving in the biggest expanse of meadow and marshland in the Tahoe area. The birds dominate, chirping, flitting, and soaring over the landscape. Whether you love birds or not, an exploration of the enormous grassland is a heavenly hiking experience.

Start: Martis Creek Wildlife Area parking lot off CA 267
Distance: 4.2-mile loop
Hiking time: About 2.5 hours
Difficulty: Moderate due only to length
Trail surface: Dirt singletrack; boardwalk
Best seasons: Late spring, summer, fall
Other trail users: Trail runners, mountain bikers on the Tomkins Memorial Trail (not permitted on the Martis Creek Trail)
Trail amenities: Information kiosk with maps; picnic facilities
Canine compatibility: Leashed dogs permitted on the Tomkins Memorial Trail. Please pick up after your pet; bags are provided at the trailhead. Do not leave bags along the trail.
Fees and permits: None
Schedule: Sunrise–sunset daily

Maps: USGS Martis Peak and Truckee CA; maps are also posted at the trailhead and along the route. Interpretive signs at the trailhead are also informative.
Trail contact: US Army Corps of Engineers, PO Box 2344, Truckee, CA 96161; (530) 587-8113; http://corpslakes.usace.army. mil/visitors/martiscreek
Special considerations: Avoid the fragile Martis Creek Trail if possible, which has been damaged by overuse. This route passes through an important Washoe Indian heritage area. Removal of artifacts and/or damaging historic or prehistoric sites is prohibited by law. The Army Corps of Engineers, which oversees the trail, also maintains a campground across CA 267, north of the wildlife area.

Finding the trailhead: From the signalized junction of CA 28 and CA 267 in Kings Beach, follow CA 267 for 8.3 miles, over Brockway summit, to the signed Martis Creek Wildlife Area turnoff on the left (south). Follow the gravel access road for 0.1 mile to the trailhead. From I-80 in Truckee, take exit 188B/CA 267 toward Kings Beach, and head south for 3 miles, past the main entrance for Martis Creek Lake, to the trailhead access road on the right. Parking is limited; if spaces are full, park along the access road or visit another day. GPS: N39 18.096' / W120 07.840'

The Hike

Willow-lined Martis Creek cuts a sinuous path through acres of wetland meadow southeast of Truckee, carving deep into the turf, its branches watering a springtime bloom of wild-flowers and providing sustenance for a variety of creatures.

The birds are most prominent, their songs loud enough to be heard over the hum of cars passing on the nearby highway. Songbirds flit from willow to rose to thatch of grass in flashes of brown, black, red, yellow, and sometimes vivid blue; watch for raptors stilling in the clear mountain air and swallows shooting in and out of the highway underpass. Fish, amphibians, and mammals large and small also call the Martis Creek Wildlife Area home.

The Tomkins Memorial Trail arcs through the sanctuary in a long loop that first immerses hikers in the meadow ecosystem, then in the forest that cloaks the slopes of the Lookout Peak, home of the Northstar ski area. The hospitable meadowland has known human habitation for 10,000 years or more, but the nature of that habitation has changed profoundly over the centuries. Where once you may have walked among hunters and gatherers, these days you will never be far from modern civilization, whether

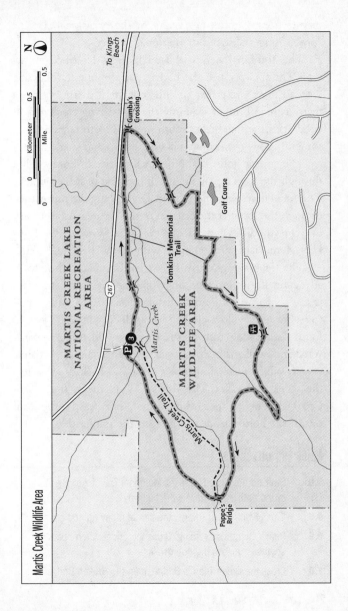

Martis Creek Wildlife Area

private homes, puttering golfers, or the occasional airplane approaching or leaving the regional airport.

The Tomkins Memorial Trail loop is described clockwise. The trail parallels the highway at the outset, following a broad track easily shared with other trail users. At one of many named bridges spanning the wandering creek and its tributaries, the trail breaks south toward Northstar, traversing sometimes soggy meadow via boardwalks and singletrack.

The metal roofs of Northstar's private homes glint through the trees as you approach the base of the mountain. The trail curves west along the edge of the golf course, then through the forest at the bottom of the ski area. A brief foray into the woodland ends back in the meadow, where the Tomkins Memorial Trail hitches up with the Martis Creek Trail.

The track along Martis Creek has been, according to its advocates, loved into near oblivion. The onetime cattle path is the subject of ongoing rehabilitation efforts, with access to its eroding, willow-choked banks discouraged. It's best to finish the meadow tour on the Tomkins Trail, using a boardwalk and well-maintained track. A bench along this final stretch offers hikers a chance to rest and look down across the creek and valley. The Tomkins Trail meets the Martis Creek Trail below the parking area; a short, easy climb leads out of the bottomlands and back to the trailhead.

Miles and Directions

0.0   Start on the signed Tomkins Memorial Trail, following the broad path that parallels the highway.

0.5   Cross Frank's Fish Bridge, the first of many named spans.

0.8   Reach Gumba's Crossing. Cross the bridge, then head southeast across the boardwalk.

1.0   Cross the Green Team's Bridge, then the Broken Bridge.

1.4   Pass under power lines and curl north as the trail runs along the fenced boundary between the wildlife area and the golf course.

1.6   At a break in the fence, marked by a trail sign, go right (northwest) to continue the loop. The left-hand path leads up into the neighborhood.

1.9   Pass a picnic table shaded by massive twin Jeffrey pines, then cross Michael Cousin's Bridge.

2.2   Now in woodland, pass several junctions with social trails leading back into the neighborhood. Stay right (southwest) at the junctions on the obvious Tomkins Memorial Trail.

2.6   A picnic table and trail map at the edge of a small meadow mark a sharp turn in the trail.

2.9   Reach a bench at the interface between meadow and woodland.

3.1   Pass through scrubland to another trail sign. Ignore side trails, staying straight (west) on the broad main track.

3.3   Arrive at Pappe's Bridge, where there is a picnic table and a trail sign. Take the Tomkins Memorial Trail, which continues straight (west) via a boardwalk. The signed Martis Creek Trail breaks to the right (northeast).

4.1   Meet the Martis Creek Trail below the trailhead and climb toward the parking area.

4.2   Arrive back at the trailhead.

4 Tahoe Meadows Interpretive Loop

Meandering through a lovely meadow beneath the summits of Slide Mountain and Mount Rose, this flat, friendly interpretive route is perfect for families, wildflower enthusiasts, and view seekers.

Start: Tahoe Rim trailhead parking lot, just off NV 431 below the Mount Rose crest
Distance: 1.3-mile loop
Hiking time: About 1 hour
Difficulty: Easy
Trail surface: Wide dirt pathway; bridges
Best seasons: Summer, fall
Other trail users: None
Trail amenities: Information signs, restrooms (open in summer)
Canine compatibility: Leashed dogs permitted
Fees and permits: None
Schedule: Sunrise–sunset daily

Maps: USGS Mount Rose NV; Tom Harrison Recreation Map of Lake Tahoe; National Geographic 803 Lake Tahoe Basin Trail Map
Trail contact: US Forest Service Lake Tahoe Basin Management Unit, Forest Supervisor's Office, 35 College Dr., South Lake Tahoe, CA 96150; (530) 543-2600; www.fs.usda.gov/ltbmu. Tahoe Rim Trail Association, 128 Market St., Suite 3E/PO Box 3267, Stateline, NV 89449; (775) 298-4485; tahoerimtrail.org.
Other: The route lies within the Humboldt-Toiyabe National Forest.

Finding the trailhead: From the intersection of NV 28 and Village Boulevard in Incline Village, head west on NV 28 to NV 431 (the scenic Mount Rose Highway). Go right (northeast) onto NV 431 for 7.3 miles to the signed trailhead on the right (east). From Tahoe City, follow CA 28 (which becomes NV 28 once you cross the state line in Crystal Bay) for 14 miles to the junction with NV 431. Turn left (north) and follow NV 431 to the trailhead parking area. If no parking is available in the lot, park in the pullout on NV 431. GPS: N39 18.433' / W119 54.436'

The Hike

Easy and scenic, the Tahoe Meadows Interpretive Loop circles through a verdant swath of grass and wildflowers at nearly 8,700 feet, offering access to stands of stately ever-greens, a chance to study a habitat that lies dormant under a thick blanket of snow for much of the year, and vistas of high ridges that stretch south to Lake Tahoe and up to the stony summits of Slide Mountain and Mount Rose. Though the Mount Rose Highway, a lovely and popular drive, is never distant, the scenery more than qualifies this as an alpine experience.

A trail sign behind the restroom marks the hike's start. The first part of the trail is accessible to hardy wheelchair users. Follow the well-groomed dirt path into the meadow; at an interpretive sign and boardwalk/bridge, the trail splits, forming the loop. Stay left (north), as the signs indicate, trav-eling in a clockwise direction.

Though the route, part of the Tahoe Rim Trail, climbs gently at the outset, it's never strenuous, making it the per-fect destination for families with toddlers just discovering the wonders of off-road treadways. The path merges into a patch of pavement, then reverts to natural surface as it traces the edge of the meadow. Altitude-stunted evergreens briefly block the meadow views, then the route traces the interface of forest and grassland as it approaches the head of the meadow.

Diverge from the Tahoe Rim Trail, which continues northeast toward Mount Rose, at a trail sign. Stay right (east) on the loop trail, curving south toward the Lake Tahoe basin

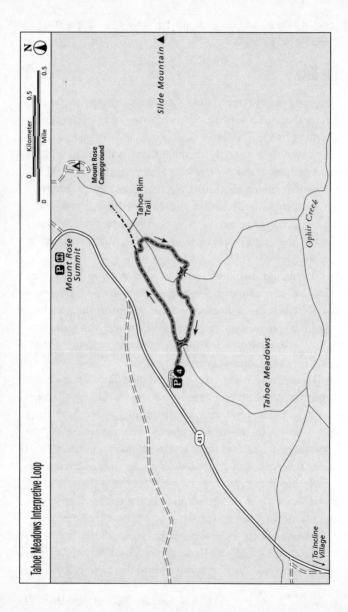

Tahoe Meadows Interpretive Loop

N

0   Kilometer   0.5

0   Mile   0.5

Mount Rose
Summit P 🏕

431

To Incline
Village

Tahoe Meadows

Tahoe Rim Trail

Mount Rose
Campground

Ophir Creek

Slide Mountain ▲

P 4

and entering a mature woodland. Interpretive signs along this stretch describe frogs and fish, butterflies and birds, human habitation and hibernation. Bridges span the stream that waters the meadow, and you can spot the tiny fish that somehow survive at these heights.

The trail emerges from the forest to cross small bridges and boardwalks in the moist meadow. Views down the mountain open into a blue void: the Tahoe basin, with the lake 2,000 feet below and out of sight. Close the loop at the bridge and trail sign, then retrace your steps back to the trailhead.

Miles and Directions

0.0   Start at the information sign.

0.1   The trail splits at an interpretive sign and bridge; take the left leg as directed by the trail sign, traveling in a clockwise direction.

0.5   Diverge from the Tahoe Rim Trail, which continues northeast toward Mount Rose. Go right (east) on the interpretive trail.

0.8   Pass a trail marker and cross a bridge.

1.2   Reach the trail junction to close the loop.

1.3   Arrive back at the trailhead.

5 Galena Falls

A lovely stretch of the Tahoe Rim Trail traverses the base of Tamarack Peak to Galena Falls, a rocky spill at the head of a willowy valley sheltered by the pink slopes of Mount Rose.

Start: Tahoe Rim Trail/Mount Rose trailhead at the summit of the Mount Rose Highway (NV 431)

Distance: 4.8 miles out and back

Hiking time: 3–4 hours

Difficulty: Moderate due to elevation and distance

Trail surface: Dirt singletrack

Best seasons: Summer, fall

Other trail users: None

Trail amenities: Parking, restrooms, picnic facilities, trash cans, informational signboards

Canine compatibility: Dogs must be on leash within 1 mile of the trailhead. Dogs are permitted in the Mount Rose Wilderness; owners must keep them under control and clean up their waste.

Fees and permits: None

Schedule: Sunrise–sunset daily

Maps: USGS Mount Rose CA; National Geographic 803 Lake Tahoe Basin Trail Map

Trail contact: US Forest Service Lake Tahoe Basin Management Unit, Forest Supervisor's Office, 35 College Dr., South Lake Tahoe, CA 96150; (530) 543-2600; www.fs.usda.gov/ltbmu. Tahoe Rim Trail Association, 128 Market St., Suite 3E/PO Box 3267, Stateline, NV 89449; (775) 298-4485; tahoerimtrail.org.

Finding the trailhead: From the junction of NV 28 and NV 431 (the Mount Rose Highway) in Incline Village (at the roundabout), go north on NV 431. Travel the scenic highway for 8 miles to the summit parking area. The trailhead is located behind the restrooms and informational signboards. GPS: N39 18.790' / W119 53.859'

The Hike

Mount Rose is an obvious hiker's target. It is among the highest ramparts of the Carson Range and, with its neighbor Slide Mountain, is an iconic element of the Lake Tahoe basin's north rim. But tucked away near the base of the mountain climb is another, easier goal: Galena Falls, a whitewater cascade about 50 feet high.

Located at about 9,000 feet on the Tahoe Rim Trail, the falls are at the head of the Galena Creek drainage. Flowing eastward, the creek waters a widening meadow of willow and wildflowers before it begins its long tumble into Reno, more than 4,000 feet below. Mount Rose, a long-extinct volcano with distinctive pink-hued slopes, towers to the northeast.

The hike begins with an easy, relatively flat traverse on the Tahoe Rim Trail (TRT). Circling southward for a stretch, skimming the flanks of Tamarack Peak, views open across marshy Tahoe Meadows toward the lake basin. Highway noise drifts up to the route, but once you top a knoll and begin to hike along northeast-facing slopes through the woods, you won't be able to discern the hum of engines from the wind ruffling the treetops.

The north- and east-facing slopes of Tamarack may hold snow late in the season, which is the only challenge hikers may face on the long, rolling traverse through thick evergreens. Openings in the woods allow great views down steep ravines into the Truckee Meadows. A short, distinctively lumpy cliff face is visible to the right (east) at about the halfway point; the route gently descends from here toward the falls.

The trail has a distinctly wild feel by the time you reach the junction of the TRT to Relay Peak and the trail to the

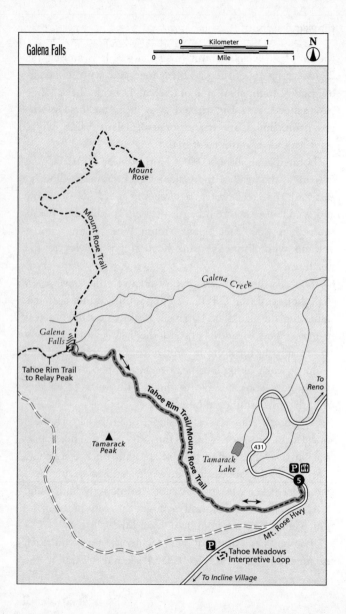

Galena Falls

| 0 | Kilometer | 1 |
| 0 | Mile | 1 |

N

Mount Rose

Mount Rose Trail

Galena Creek

Galena Falls

Tahoe Rim Trail to Relay Peak

Tahoe Rim Trail/Mount Rose Trail

To Reno

431

Tamarack Peak

Tamarack Lake

P

5

Mt. Rose Hwy

P Tahoe Meadows Interpretive Loop

To Incline Village

summit of Mount Rose. Galena Falls, vigorous in early season and mellowing as the summer draws on, tumbles down a broken rock face, the stone brown and blocky behind the cascade. Visit in late spring and early summer for the best wildflower display in the meadow. Find a seat on a dry rock and enjoy the falls and flowers before returning as you came.

Miles and Directions

0.0   Start at the Mount Rose trailhead at the summit parking area on NV 431, following the Tahoe Rim Trail and the signed trail to Mount Rose.

0.1   At the trail Y (the junction of the Tahoe Rim Trail heading south into Tahoe Meadows), go right (up the stairs) on the TRT/Mount Rose Trail.

0.5   Top a knoll and check out the views south across Lake Tahoe and northeast into the Truckee Meadows and Washoe Valley.

1.4   Round a knob with views of a lumpy, wooded ridge.

2.4   Reach Galena Falls and the junction of the TRT to Relay Peak and the trail to Mount Rose. This is the turnaround point, though if you desire you can continue on to the summit of Mount Rose, or follow the TRT along the lake basin rim. Otherwise, return as you came.

4.8   Arrive back at the trailhead.

Options: For those who crave summits, the top of Mount Rose appears tantalizingly close. Another 2.4 miles of incessant climbing along the well-marked Mount Rose Trail leads to the apex, where the panoramic views into Nevada and down onto Lake Tahoe are superlative. Be prepared for a long, hard hike, however; there's not only mileage to consider but also altitude. The summit is at 10,776 feet, and the climbing doesn't let up beyond Galena Falls.

If you are staying in Incline Village, the best close-in option for a quick leg stretch or workout is the Incline Village Exercise Course, which follows a winding route through a patch of forest just off Ski Beach. This 1.1-mile loop is lined with exercise stations and navigates a strip of forest between a pair of streams. While not a wilderness hike, given that the Village Green, the Hyatt Regency hotel, and private homes are visible from the trail, the pocket of woodland provides a nice quick escape. Start at the signed trailhead at the Aspen Grove Community Center on Lakeshore Boulevard (GPS: N39 14.410' / W119 56.746'). A network of walking trails also follows Lakeshore Drive and winds through the neighborhoods of the village. Mostly paved, these paths connect businesses, schools, and recreation sites.

Midway between the mountaintop and the beach lies another North Shore option. The Incline Downhill is popular with both hikers and mountain bikers, and it offers great lake views, a stretch along a vibrant mountain stream, and a thigh-pumping climb. Because there's no easy parking at the base of the trail in Incline, most hikers do this route either upside-down, or one-way, starting at the trailhead on the Mount Rose Highway and ending in Incline, where they've left a shuttle car. The route is 5.5 miles out and back (2.75 miles as a shuttle), follows a dirt trail, and dogs are permitted. The upper trailhead is in a parking pullout 3.9 miles up NV 431 from its junction with NV 28 in Incline Village (GPS: N39 16.115' / W119 55.835').

6 Sand Harbor Nature Trail

Take a quick stroll along the boardwalk at Sand Harbor and indulge in unimpeded views across Lake Tahoe. The path also hooks around rocky shoreline coves, and interpretive signs describe some of the components that make the lake's environment beautiful and unique. The loop is perfect for families.

Start: Informational kiosk near the restrooms at Sand Harbor
Distance: 0.4-mile loop
Hiking time: About 30 minutes
Difficulty: Easy
Trail surface: Boardwalk and brick walkway
Best seasons: Spring, summer, fall
Other trail users: None
Trail amenities: Restrooms, water, visitor center, gift shop, trash cans
Canine compatibility: Dogs not permitted
Fees and permits: Day-use fee
Schedule: The park is open from 8 a.m. to 9 p.m. daily from Memorial Day to Labor Day. From May 1 to Memorial Day and from Labor Day to Sept 30, hours are from 8 a.m. to 7 p.m. From Oct 1 to Apr 30, hours are from 8 a.m. to 5 p.m.
Maps: USGS Marlette Lake NV, but no map is needed.
Trail contact: Lake Tahoe–Nevada State Park, PO Box 6116, Incline Village, NV 89452; (775) 831-0494; parks.nv.gov/parks/sand-harbor/
Other: Sand Harbor accommodates swimming, boating, and picnic facilities. The park also hosts the annual Lake Tahoe Shakespeare Festival in late summer; the amphitheater is cupped inside the trail loop. Sand Harbor is also a popular spot for scuba diving in the lake, with wetsuit-clad divers exploring the underwater rock formations.
Special considerations: The trail is wheelchair accessible. The parking lots fill by midmorning on summer days, restricting access to the park and trail. The Tahoe Transportation District runs a shuttle between Sand Harbor and Incline Village daily during the high season; visit tahoetransportation.org/eastshore express for details.

Finding the trailhead: From the junction of NV 28 and Village Boulevard in Incline Village, follow NV 28 south along Lake Tahoe's east shore for 4.8 miles to the signed park entrance on the right (west). GPS: N39 11.849' / W119 55.886'

The Hike

Visit Sand Harbor early in the day and you'll find the typically crowded beach nearly deserted, though the parking lot may bustle with divers preparing to explore the nearby shoreline. You'll also likely have the boardwalk that circles Sand Point all to yourself, a rare treat sweetened with amazing vistas. On a typical summer morning, the smooth lake surface reflects a sky of uninterrupted blue, and the low sun casts defining shadows on rock formations cluttering the lakeshore.

But while a morning walk holds special appeal, the Sand Harbor Nature Trail is delightful at any time of day. Super-easy, wheelchair and stroller accessible, and lined with interpretive signs, the route is a fine addition to any East Shore visit.

Begin on the north side of the restrooms at an informational kiosk, stepping onto an elevated walkway constructed of recycled plastic boards. The boardwalk overlooks a small rocky cove where divers enter the cold water and kayakers launch. Ponderosa pines, snow fences, interpretive signs, and jumbles of granite line the route.

As you round Sand Point (traveling counterclockwise), the trail surface changes to brick, and short side trails lead to vista points overlooking tiny coves guarded by granite boulders. The last section of the trail looks down on the huge sandy beach, often thickly blanketed with sunbathers and colorful shade umbrellas. The trail ends in front of the

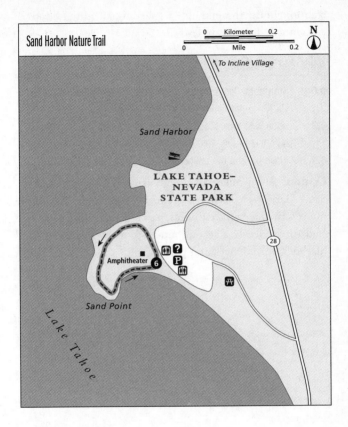

restrooms near the entrance to the amphitheater, home of the annual Shakespeare festival.

Miles and Directions

0.0   Start at the kiosk on the north side of the restrooms, traveling the loop in a counterclockwise direction.

0.2   Short side trails lead to vista points. Explore the shoreline, returning to the main trail and continuing the circuit.

0.4   Arrive back at the trailhead.

Option: A 0.6-mile trail along Lake Tahoe's shoreline links Sand Harbor to Memorial Point, where you'll find more interpretive signage, restrooms, parking, and short paths that lead to overlooks. The out-and-back route begins in Sand Harbor's north/boat ramp parking lot.

7 Skunk Harbor

An unfortunate name for a favorite trail, Skunk Harbor is no stinker. Instead, a broad, steep track leads to a secluded bay where Tahoe's clear water washes in a rainbow arc onto a crescent beach, melting from indigo to turquoise to gold as it approaches the shore.

Start: Unmarked turnout on the lake side of NV 28. Look for a green gate.

Distance: 3.0 miles out and back

Hiking time: About 2 hours

Difficulty: Moderate due to elevation change of more than 600 feet

Trail surface: Dirt access road

Best seasons: Late spring, summer, fall

Other trail users: The occasional mountain biker

Trail amenities: None. Limited parking (for about 5 cars) is at the gate/trailhead, with parking for 10–12 more cars in a paved pullout about 100 yards north (uphill) of the gate.

Canine compatibility: Leashed dogs permitted

Fees and permits: None

Schedule: Sunrise–sunset daily

Maps: USGS Marlette Lake (NV); Lake Tahoe Basin Management Unit Map; National Geographic 803 Lake Tahoe Basin Trail Map; Tom Harrison Recreation Map of Lake Tahoe

Trail contact: US Forest Service Lake Tahoe Basin Management Unit, Forest Supervisor's Office, 35 College Dr., South Lake Tahoe, CA 96150; (530) 543-2600; www.fs.usda.gov/ltbmu

Other: Limited parking and the lack of signage make the trailhead a challenge to find but ensure that the route will not be crowded.

Finding the trailhead: From the junction of NV 28 and Village Boulevard in Incline Village, follow NV 28 south along the east shore for 9.3 miles to the unsigned trailhead on the right (west/

lakeside). From the intersection of US 50 and CA 89 in South Lake Tahoe, drive 17.9 miles north on US 50 to its intersection with NV 28 near Spooner Summit. Turn left (north) onto NV 28 and go about 2.4 miles to the trailhead, which is on the left side of the highway. A green gate tucked below the highway blocks vehicle access to the trail. GPS: N39 07.717' / W119 55.878'

The Hike

As if a sandy beach, sunbaked rocks, and cool, clear water weren't enough to draw hikers down to Skunk Harbor, the little cove is also the site of the picturesque Newhall House, built in 1923 as a wedding gift from George Newhall to his wife, Caroline. A plaque explains the origin and preservation of the house, but the true monument is the rustic structure itself, all stonework and peaked roofs and heavy wooden window frames. Peek through barred windows into the bare interior, then spread a picnic on one of the verandas, enjoying wonderful views that open through the harbor onto the lake.

Swimming and picnicking are popular activities for all who venture down the steep access road to the harbor. Powerboats sometimes drop anchor in the cove, sharing the amenities with those who've arrived on foot. But even with some coming by land and others by water, the destination is seldom crowded. An "upside-down" hike, with the climb on the return trip, Skunk Harbor allows you to prepare for the ascent by enjoying a long lakeside rest.

To begin, pass the gate and head down on the paved, then dirt, roadway. The old road flattens and circles through a drainage, then traverses the mountainside. From the traverse you can catch views of Slaughterhouse Canyon and the lake beyond.

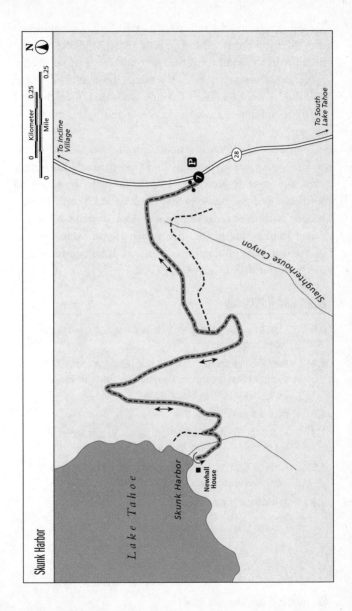

Skunk Harbor

Lake Tahoe

Skunk Harbor

Newhall
House

Slaughterhouse Canyon

P
7

28

To Incline
Village

To South
Lake Tahoe

N

Kilometer   0.25
0

Mile   0.25
0

When you reach the unsigned trail fork with the road into Slaughterhouse Canyon, stay right (straight) on the broad road to Skunk Harbor. The route drops more steeply, rounding a switchback and passing through a clearing. Another switchback loops through woodland, then the trail narrows and enters a swampy area watered by an ephemeral stream.

Just beyond the moist patch, the trail forks. Go left (west) and meander down through lush undergrowth, crossing a streamlet, to the Newhall House. Footpaths lead around to the side of the house facing the lake and Skunk Harbor proper, with the pilings of a ruined dock stretching into the water. Explore the beach, then return as you came, keeping in mind that it's all uphill from the bay. It takes a bit longer to climb out than it does to descend.

Miles and Directions

0.0   Start by passing the green gate and heading down the broad access road.

0.4   Pass the junction with the trail that leads left (down and south) to Slaughterhouse Canyon. Stay right (down and west) on the road to Skunk Harbor.

1.0   Round a switchback.

1.4   Reach the T junction above the harbor. Beach access trails are to the right (north); the house is to the left (south).

1.5   Arrive at the house and beach. Rest and relax at the waterside, then retrace your steps.

3.0   Arrive back at the trailhead.

8 Spooner Lake Loop

Once a water source for miners working silver mines near Virginia City, Spooner Lake is now the gateway to Lake Tahoe–Nevada State Park's Spooner Backcountry and is the centerpiece of a splendid short hike that circumnavigates its shoreline.

Start: Main parking lot for Lake Tahoe–Nevada State Park

Distance: 2.1-mile loop

Hiking time: About 1.5 hours

Difficulty: Easy

Trail surface: Singletrack, dirt roadway, and pavement

Best seasons: Late spring, summer, fall (when the aspens turn)

Other trail users: None on the loop itself; cyclists on the portions leading to and from the loop

Trail amenities: Parking, restrooms, water, information, picnic areas, Spooner Summit Rental Concession (offering mountain bike rentals). The park also hosts backcountry cabins and walk-in primitive camping.

Canine compatibility: Leashed dogs permitted

Fees and permits: Day-use fee

Schedule: The park is open from 8 a.m. to 9 p.m. daily from Memorial Day to Labor Day. From May 1 to Memorial Day and from Labor Day to Sept 30, hours are from 8 a.m. to 7 p.m. From Oct 1 to Apr 30, hours are from 8 a.m. to 5 p.m.

Maps: USGS Glenbrook (NV); state park map available at the entrance station; information board map at the trailhead

Trail contact: Lake Tahoe–Nevada State Park, PO Box 6116, Incline Village, NV 89452; (775) 831-0494; parks.nv.gov/parks/marlette-hobart-backcountry

Finding the trailhead: From the junction of NV 28 and Village Boulevard in Incline Village, follow NV 28 south for about 11 miles to the signed turnoff into Lake Tahoe–Nevada State Park. Turn left (east) into the park and follow the park road to the trailhead. From South

Lake Tahoe/Stateline, follow US 50 north for about 12 miles to the junction with NV 28. Go left (west) onto NV 28 for 0.5 mile to the park entrance on the right. GPS: N39 06.369' / W119 54.963'

The Hike

Glades of quaking aspen, their chattering leaves bright green in spring and vivid gold in fall, crowd the first mile of this flat circuit around Spooner Lake. The aspen groves, some featuring gnarly old specimens with thick trunks scarred by graffiti, blend into an evergreen woodland on the lake's northern shores, with wildflowers sprinkled in meadow grasses flourishing in small clearings. Breaks in the trees allow views across the water, where ducks and other waterfowl are virtually guaranteed to be swimming and spotting an osprey is possible.

The large information sign at the trailhead—the first of a series of interpretive signs scattered along the loop—shows the extensive trail system that explores the backcountry surrounding Marlette Lake and Hobart Reservoir. Spooner Lake offers a sampling of what you'd find farther in.

Interpretive signs also detail how the lake was integrated into the complex water and lumber delivery systems that fed resources from the Sierra to the silver mines on Nevada's high desert. An amazing array of railroads, haul roads, and flumes (one 17 miles long) originating around Lake Tahoe carried water and timber to the mines, with Spooner Lake, then part of Spooner Ranch, strategically located near the east-side summit. The ranch owner, Michel Spooner, along with a partner, established Spooner Station in 1860, with a mill, hotel, saloon, and more accommodating the needs of miners, lumberjacks, and travelers.

From the trailhead follow the paved, interpretive Beetle Discovery Trail down through a boulder-bordered picnic

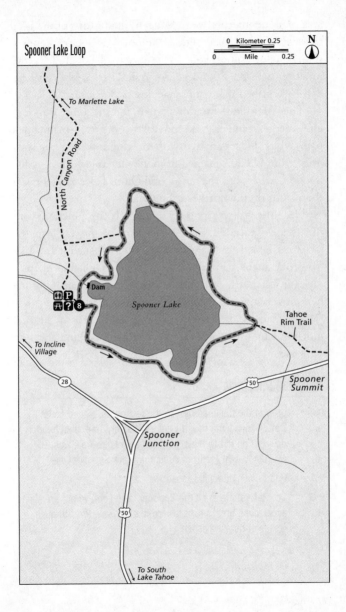

area; trailside interpretive signs detail the history of the lake, the wildlife and plant life it supports, and cross-country skiing opportunities. Follow the dirt road downhill to the junction with the Spooner Lake Trail. The loop begins here and is described in a counterclockwise direction.

The ecotones—meadow, aspen forest, coniferous forest—merge seamlessly as you follow the well-maintained path, which is accessorized with viewing benches. Highway noise from US 50, screened from view by trees, can be a distraction at first, but the automobile hum fades as you reach the woods on the northern shoreline.

Near the halfway point you'll reach the junction with the Tahoe Rim Trail; follow a section of the TRT to the lake's earthen dam. Many of the anglers that visit the lake hang out at the dam, with rocky beaches suitable for picnicking just north of the structure. The bugs can be brutal here in season; walk with your mouth closed!

The dam is also where the loop closes. From the trail junction, climb through the woods to the parking area and trailhead.

Miles and Directions

0.0 Start at the trailhead next to the restrooms, signed for "All Trails." Follow the paved Beetle Discovery Trail, then head downhill on dirt to the signed Spooner Lake Trail, where you'll stay right (east) to circumnavigate Spooner Lake.

0.1 Head down through a meadow.

0.6 Stay left (straight) on the Spooner Lake Loop where an access trail breaks right toward the highway. Pass through groves of quaking aspen.

1.0 Cross a boardwalk over the inlet stream and climb to the junction with the Tahoe Rim Trail. Go left (southwest) on the signed TRT/Spooner Lake Loop.

1.6 At the junction with the link to the North Canyon Road to Marlette Lake, stay left (south), following the lake's shoreline.

1.8 Arrive at the dam and a trail junction. Cross the dam and go down through the spillway. Pass a signboard listing angling regulations, then cross the gravel road to the sign that points uphill to the parking area. Two paths lead through the woods; pick one and start the short climb.

2.1 Arrive back at the trailhead.

Options: Miles of trails head north into the Marlette-Hobart backcountry from the Spooner Lake trailhead. For the hardier hiker, a fine 10-mile lollipop loop leads from Spooner Lake to Marlette Lake and back. After a brief walk along the aspen-lined North Canyon Road, which you'll share with mountain bikers, a hikers-only trail breaks left and traverses up past the remnants of an old woodcutter's cabin, then on to Marlette Lake, which is big, blue, and inviting. You can return as you came, or follow North Canyon Road back down to the trailhead, forming a loop. The famous Flume Trail can also be reached from the backcountry: A mountain biker's favorite, this route doesn't see much foot traffic.

The Tahoe Rim Trail also can be reached from nearby Spooner Summit, located a short distance up NV 28 and US 50 from the park entrance. From the summit the TRT heads north to Snow Valley Peak and beyond; heading south, it skirts Duane Bliss Peak and continues to Kingsbury Grade and beyond. Walking north or south on the TRT for 2 to 3 miles from the summit offers off-the-beaten-path

opportunities for the day hiker. While there aren't spectacular destinations, other than the occasional vista point offering
views down onto the lake or onto the Nevada desert, these
stretches of trail make for peaceful walks in the woods.

9 Five Lakes Trail

The surprise of summertime at a ski area reveals beauty viewed through a different lens. And it requires effort: Slopes traversed easily when covered with snow require work when their rocky bases are revealed—and you have to hike up them as well as come down. The climb to Five Lakes offers access (not lift-served) to the slopes near Alpine Meadows, then mellows in the shady forest surrounding the first of the Five Lakes.

Start: Signed trailhead alongside Deer Park Drive

Distance: 4.2 miles out and back

Hiking time: 2–3 hours

Difficulty: More challenging due to 1,000-foot elevation gain. The trail is mostly shadeless and can be hot.

Trail surface: Dirt singletrack

Best seasons: Late spring, summer mornings, fall

Other trail users: None

Trail amenities: None

Canine compatibility: Dogs permitted except where posted in the Granite Chief Wilderness

Fees and permits: None

Schedule: Sunrise–sunset daily

Maps: USGS Tahoe City and Granite Chief CA; Lake Tahoe Basin Management Unit Map; National Geographic 803 Lake Tahoe Basin Trail Map

Trail contact: Tahoe National Forest, Truckee Ranger District, 10811 Stockrest Springs Rd., Truckee, CA 96161; (530) 587-3558; www.fs.usda.gov/tahoe. US Forest Service Lake Tahoe Basin Management Unit, Forest Supervisor's Office, 35 College Dr., South Lake Tahoe, CA 96150; (530) 543-2600; www.fs.usda.gov/ltbmu.

Special considerations: Given the elevation gain and exposure, do not attempt the hike if you have heart, respiratory, or knee problems.

Finding the trailhead: From the intersection of CA 89 and CA 28 in Tahoe City, follow CA 89 northwest (toward Truckee) for 3.6 miles. Turn left (west) onto Alpine Meadows Road and go 2.2 miles to the trailhead, which is across from the second intersection with Deer Park Drive. Limited parking is available along Alpine Meadows Road. GPS: N39 10.749' / W120 13.790'

The Hike

Three distinct settings, and thus three distinct moods, lie along the trail to Five Lakes. The most arduous part of the trek is at the outset, where switchbacks climb through a sun-fed thicket of manzanita, mule ear, and snowberry. The second section features great views of the Alpine Meadows Ski Area, metal ski lift towers punched into smooth, colorful granite slabs, as well as an exposed traverse of a shallow granite-walled canyon. On the short third leg, a thick fir forest takes over, obscuring views and hiding all but one of the five small lakes that nestle in the shade.

As for the moods—well, the first pitch is just plain vexing, the second pitch exhilarates with its great views, and the third is peaceful and contemplative.

Begin by climbing switchbacks on the mountainside north of Bear Creek. Switchbacks and more switchbacks . . . keep climbing until you leave the scrub behind. The terrain becomes more alpine as you ascend, and views open down-canyon toward the Truckee River valley and up-canyon onto the slopes of the Alpine Meadows Ski Area.

Traverse to yet another switchback, then climb under ski lift towers into a saddle, where the trail enters a narrowing side canyon with black-streaked walls. Two switchbacks are built like giant stair steps into orange rock; beyond, the trail traverses above the shallowing canyon to more gentle

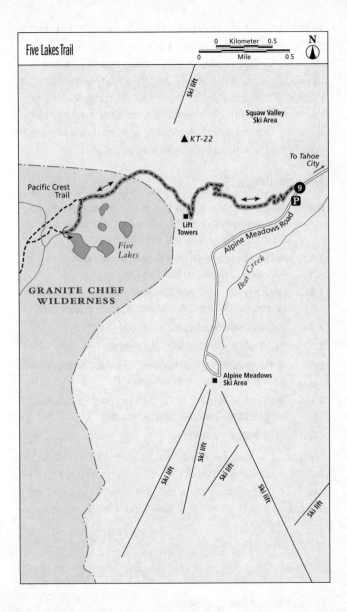

Five Lakes Trail

0 Kilometer 0.5

0 Mile 0.5

N

Squaw Valley
Ski Area

▲ KT-22

Ski lift

To Tahoe
City

Pacific Crest
Trail

9
P

Lift
Towers

Alpine Meadows Road

Bear Creek

Five
Lakes

GRANITE CHIEF
WILDERNESS

Alpine Meadows
Ski Area

Ski lift

Ski lift

Ski lift

Ski lift

Ski lift

switchbacks. At the outskirts of the fir forest, a sign denotes the boundary of the Granite Chief Wilderness.

Trails collide in the woods. At the signed junction with the Pacific Crest Trail (PCT), go left (south) to the shoreline of one of the small lakes, where social trails lead to inviting rest spots on the water. You'll have to bushwhack and do some clever off-trail navigating to find the other nearby lakes. Visit for a time, then return as you came.

Miles and Directions

0.0   Start at the "Granite Chief Wilderness" trail sign. It's all uphill from here, with switchbacks and granite stair steps aiding in the ascent. Take it slow and enjoy the views.

1.1   Pass under several ski area lift towers (you'll wish you could commandeer a chair by this point).

1.2   Cross a small saddle and curve into a granite-walled side canyon, passing a trail marker and a private property sign.

1.4   Negotiate switchbacks carved into orange rock.

1.7   Pass the "Granite Chief Wilderness" sign.

2.0   At the signed junction of the Five Lakes Trail and the PCT to Whiskey Creek Camp, stay left (south).

2.1   Reach the shoreline of one of the Five Lakes. The others can't be seen. This is the turnaround point.

4.2   Arrive back at the trailhead.

Option: The trail continues through a meadow and on to a second junction with the PCT at 2.5 miles. From there you can hike or backpack to Whiskey Creek Camp and other destinations in the Granite Chief Wilderness.

10 Shirley Canyon Cascades

Squaw Creek rambles down a steep canyon from the heights of Granite Chief and Solitude to the Squaw Valley ski resort's busy village. A trail climbs more than 1,300 feet from the base to the top of the resort's aerial tram but, to keep it easy, this route takes you as far as a set of lovely cascades.

Start: Signed trailhead at the junction of Squaw Peak Road and Squaw Peak Way

Distance: 1.5 miles out and back (or more)

Hiking time: 1–2 hours

Difficulty: Moderate due to route finding

Trail surface: Faint dirt and rock pathway marked with blue blazes

Best seasons: Late spring and early summer, when snowmelt fills the creek

Other trail users: None

Trail amenities: Information signboard

Canine compatibility: Leashed dogs permitted (though they often run off-leash)

Fees and permits: None

Schedule: Sunrise–sunset daily

Maps: USGS Tahoe City and Granite Chief CA; Lake Tahoe Basin Management Unit Map; National Geographic 803 Lake Tahoe Basin Trail Map

Trail contact: Squaw Valley Resort, 1960 Squaw Valley Rd./PO Box 2007, Olympic Valley, CA 96146; (800) 403-0206 or (530) 452-4331; squawalpine.com. US Forest Service Lake Tahoe Basin Management Unit, Forest Supervisor's Office, 35 College Dr., South Lake Tahoe, CA 96150; (530) 543-2600; www.fs.usda.gov/ltbmu.

Finding the trailhead: From the intersection of CA 89 and CA 28 in Tahoe City, follow CA 89 northwest (toward Truckee) for 5 miles. Turn left (west) onto Squaw Valley Road and go 2.5 miles, past the huge village parking lot, to Squaw Peak Road. Turn right onto Squaw Peak Road and follow it for 0.4 mile to its junction with Squaw Peak

Way. Limited parking is available alongside both Squaw Peak Road and Squaw Peak Way. GPS: N39 11.910' / W120 14.480'

The Hike

Squaw Valley Resort can be as busy in summer as it is in winter. The aerial tram runs daily, offering access to High Camp, with its pool, skating rink, restaurant and bar, and access to hiking trails that skim along the high ridges overlooking the Truckee River valley and the Tahoe basin.

But just beyond the bustling village, the trail up Shirley Canyon offers a quiet change of pace. The path is rustic almost from the start: no wide, crushed gravel treadways or boardwalks to keep you on track. Instead, the singletrack climbs alongside Squaw Creek, which rocks and rolls in a meltwater rush in late spring and early summer. The destination is a small waterfall and a series of cascades that mist the trail and those who travel on it.

Begin by passing behind the large, obvious information signboard, which shows a map of the route. The trail is obvious at first, but grows indistinct as it meanders up into the steep-walled canyon. Watch for blue blazes painted on rocks, which show the way, and stay left of the creek. While the path unceasingly ascends, the real challenge is in picking the most comfortable/obvious way forward.

Pass a trail marker, then reach the first cascade/waterfall at 0.3 mile. You can turn around here or continue uphill to a second tumble. If you choose to continue, pass another trail marker and then bear left through the woods on a nice, straightforward stretch of trail along the left side of the creek. Where paths diverge at about 0.8 mile, stay left, then cross a granite slab (follow the blue blazes) to another

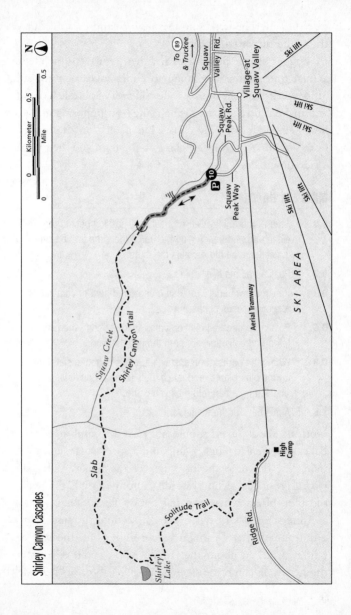

Shirley Canyon Cascades

cascade view. The trail continues upward and onward, but this is the turnaround point.

Higher up, the path leaves and then returns to the creek a final time before beginning to climb in earnest toward Shirley Lake and the Squaw Valley ski area's Solitude basin. If you make it up the crux of the route—an imposing granite headwall—you not only earn a lunch spot on the Shirley Lake shoreline but can also climb to the tram and then hitch a ride down.

Miles and Directions

0.0 Start at the Shirley Canyon trailhead, passing behind the signboard and heading up the trail. Where the trail becomes indistinct, blue blazes mark the route.

0.2 Pass a trail marker.

0.3 Reach the waterfall. You can turn around here or continue to a second series of cascades.

0.5 Pass a second trail marker, cross a side stream, then stay left on a straightforward path through the woods.

0.8 Where the paths diverge, stay left, cross a granite slab following blue blazes, and reach the second cascade view. Check it out, then return as you came.

1.5 Arrive back at the trailhead.

Option: Hardy hikers should not miss the climb to Shirley Lake, and then to High Camp and a spectacular (and free) tram ride down to the base area of the Squaw Valley ski resort. From the second cascade, continue uphill, following the blue blazes where the trail grows faint. Steep pitches are interspersed with relatively flat sections, leading up to a trail junction at 1.3 miles where signs point the way to Shirley Lake. At about the 2-mile mark, you'll encounter the headwall; climb the steep, imposing slab on its left side, again following blue blazes and the occasional rock cairn. Top out and proceed through woodland to Shirley Lake and the Solitude basin (with ski lift) at 3.25 miles. The trail to High Camp climbs a rocky slope out of the basin (follow the Solitude/High Camp trail markers), then winds up the barren slopes to the broad roadway that links back to High Camp and the aerial tram. The views from on high are panoramic, with Lake Tahoe winking blue between the ridges. Total mileage to High Camp is just more than 4 miles.

11 Antone Meadows

This wander through the woods, through a state park with no hoopla—in fact, no facilities of any kind other than trails and markers—leads to a secluded meadow frequented by deer, ducks, and not a whole lot of humans.

Start: Unsigned road that leads straight west from the parking area
Distance: 6.1-mile loop
Hiking time: 3–4 hours
Difficulty: Moderate due only to length
Trail surface: Dirt roadway, singletrack
Best seasons: Late spring, summer, fall
Other trail users: Mountain bikers, trail runners

Trail amenities: A park sign with a map
Canine compatibility: Leashed dogs permitted on fire roads, but not in the natural preserve or on the trail at Antone Meadows
Fees and permits: None
Schedule: Sunrise–sunset daily
Maps: USGS Tahoe City; Burton Creek State Park brochure and map online
Trail contact: Burton Creek State Park; www.parks.ca.gov

Finding the trailhead: From the intersection of CA 89 and CA 28 in Tahoe City, follow CA 28 north for 1.6 miles to an unsigned left turn just before Tamarack Lodge. The left turn on to Burton Creek State Park access road is almost directly opposite the road into Star Harbor. Follow the access road for 0.2 mile, staying left past Tamarack Lodge; the pavement is replaced by gravel after about 0.1 mile. Parking is in a clearing just beyond the park sign. GPS: N39 11.199' / W120 07.504'

The Hike

Burton Creek State Park, home to Antone Meadows and the preserve that protects it, is the shy sibling of the flashier state parks around Lake Tahoe. This is the park where you can come for quiet, where you can retreat for a long, peaceful walk in the woods.

That doesn't mean you'll be entirely alone, however. The dirt roads that crisscross the pine and fir forest that sprawls west of the lakeshore are popular with mountain bikers, who may ride singly or in packs but are, without fail (at least thus far), friendly and easy to share the trails with. They come and go quickly, so you'll have the trails mostly to yourself even if you have a number of encounters.

Antone Meadows, the ostensible goal of this hike, is a long stretch of flowing grasses and willow watered by Burton Creek, which meanders lazily down toward Lake Tahoe. It's a lovely spot and well worth the journey, but the journey is also the goal.

The loop begins by climbing via the dirt road that leads straight ahead (to the west) from the parking area. The steeper trail to the right (north) is the return route. After a brief uphill the road crosses a bridge spanning Burton Creek, then begins to climb again.

Pay attention to the numbers tacked onto the trees at the trail junctions; maps have been installed at these junctions as well to keep hikers, mountain bikers, and winter cross-country skiers on track. Pass a series of numbered intersections before you reach the signed singletrack trail that breaks left (west) toward Antone Meadows Natural Preserve.

The trail to the preserve is where the wandering begins—wandering mind and wandering shoes. The meadow remains out of sight until you reach its head. It dominates the right-hand side of the trail as you head east, back toward the lake. Watch the water for fowl; ducks and geese ply the shallow, curling creek.

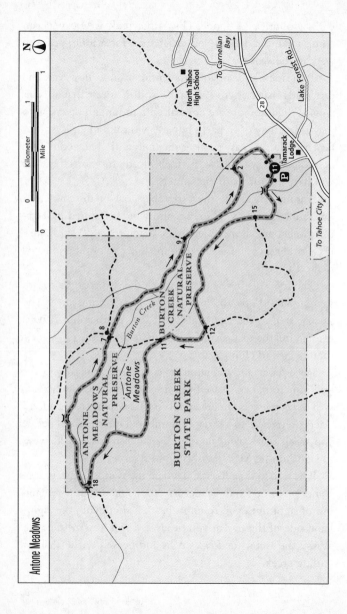

Antone Meadows

The singletrack eventually dumps you back onto dirt roadways, which are followed back down to the trailhead. Watch for views of the lake through the trees as you near trail's end, and watch your step on the steep final descent to the parking area.

Miles and Directions

0.0   Start on the dirt road that heads straight west. The steeper trail to the right (north) is the return route.

0.2   Cross the bridge over Burton Creek.

0.4   Reach trail junction 15. Stay right.

1.4   At the trail Y (with no sign), stay right; just beyond is trail junction 12, with a trail map. Stay right again.

1.8   Reach the junction with the Antone Meadows Natural Preserve Trail (trail junction 11). Take the singletrack that breaks left, away from the road.

3.0   Reach trail junction 18 at the park boundary and the head of Antone Meadows, which remains mostly out of sight until you cross the plank bridge over crystalline Burton Creek and begin heading east. The grassland, with the willow-lined creek, dominates the outset of the return leg of the loop.

4.3   Reach a five-way trail junction at junction 8; continue straight toward trail junction 7. A left turn leads into the Dollar Unit (an adjacent parcel of public land) and a right leads back to the roadway you traveled in on.

5.1   Reach trail junction 9 (again, with a map). Continue straight, paralleling Burton Creek on the downhill run. Enjoy brief lake views between this junction and the next.

5.7   At trail junction 2 (a three-way intersection), stay right, heading downhill. The left turn heads toward North Tahoe High School.

5.9   Drop down steeply off the forested bench toward the trailhead.

6.1   Arrive back at the trailhead.

12 Truckee River Trail

One of the most visible and popular trails in north Lake Tahoe, this well-maintained paved route parallels the Truckee River from Tahoe City to Alpine Meadows Road and beyond. Along the way you'll enjoy views of the sparkling river, the lush riparian habitat that lines its banks, the dark evergreen forest that blankets the valley walls, and the crowds that float the river.

Start: Signed trailhead in 64-Acres Park at the Y in Tahoe City

Distance: 7.2 miles out and back

Hiking time: 4–5 hours

Difficulty: Moderate due only to length

Trail surface: Paved bike path

Best seasons: Spring, summer, fall

Other trail users: Lots of cyclists, runners, skaters

Trail amenities: Restrooms; interpretive signs. Porta-pottys are spaced along the trail.

Canine compatibility: Leashed dogs permitted

Fees and permits: None

Schedule: Sunrise–sunset daily

Maps: USGS Tahoe City CA; Lake Tahoe Basin Management Unit Map; National Geographic 803 Lake Tahoe Basin Trail Map; Tom Harrison Recreation Map of Lake Tahoe

Trail contact: Tahoe City Public Utility District, Parks and Recreation Department, 221 Fairway Dr./PO Box 5249, Tahoe City, CA 96145; (530) 583-3796; www.tahoecitypud.com

Special considerations: The route is wheelchair accessible.

Finding the trailhead: From the signalized intersection of CA 89 and CA 28 in Tahoe City, go 0.2 mile south on CA 89 to a signed right turn into the large trailhead parking area at 64-Acres Park. GPS: N39 9.877' / W120 8.840'

The Hike

On long, hot summer days, the Truckee River swirls with the revelry of river rafters. The clear water, a rich green fading to gold in the shallows, is topped by the dazzling blues, oranges, and yellows of the rafts, and the vibrant colors of boaters' swimsuits and hats. This riotous rainbow spills onto the trail that follows the river from Tahoe City to the inn at River Run, where neon-clad cyclists and runners mingle with families in casual khaki and anglers in rubberized camouflage.

It is virtually impossible to get lost on the Truckee River Trail; if you wander into the water or find yourself sharing the asphalt with automobiles, you've strayed from the route. Mile markers are also provided. A broken yellow line down the center of the trail separates downstream traffic from those headed upstream. Proximity to the highway precludes any illusion of this being a wilderness hike, but the route makes for an entertaining family outing, and it is wheelchair accessible.

The trail begins by crossing the arcing bridge to the north shore of the river, then bears left (west), running between the watercourse and CA 89. Passage around businesses and over driveways makes for an inauspicious start, but once the trail drops waterside, dense willow forms a buffer to the roadway and sometimes hides the meandering river. The only intersections, once you leave Tahoe City, are with the driveways and private bridges of lucky souls with homes perched on the riverbanks.

Sandbars in the river offer respite for the rafters; for hikers and other trail users, narrow social paths lead to small rocky or sandy beaches that serve as viewpoints, picnic

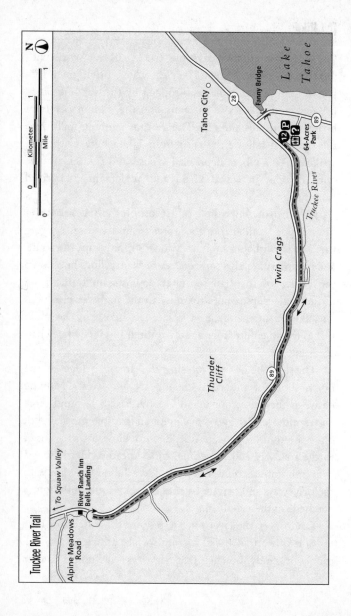

spots, or rest and turnaround spots. Hike as far as you'd like; if you have the time and energy, follow the trail all the way to Alpine Meadows Road and River Ranch. Return as you came.

Miles and Directions

0.0   Start by crossing the bridge in 64-Acres Park, then turn left (west) onto the paved bike path.

0.2   Leave the outskirts of Tahoe City behind.

1.0   Pass a mile marker.

2.0   Pass another mile marker and a "Congested Area" sign.

3.0   Pass a third mile marker and a private driveway.

3.4   Climb the only hill along the route (it's short) to the rafters' staging area.

3.6   Reach Bells Landing and the inn at River Ranch. Have a cool drink on the patio, then retrace your steps to the trailhead.

7.2   Arrive back at the trailhead.

Options: From River Run you can continue west on the Truckee River Trail to Squaw Valley Road. The total round-trip is 10 miles; maps are available at the Parks and Recreation Department office.

The Truckee River trailhead in Tahoe City also serves as the junction for other lakeshore bike paths, including the paved trail that heads north to Dollar Point, and one that follows CA 89 south to Sugar Pine Point State Park.

Finally, a nice section of the Tahoe Rim Trail (TRT) begins near downtown Tahoe City and leads about 2 miles to a vista point. To reach this part of the TRT from near the junction of CA 28 and CA 89, turn right onto Fairway Drive and go 0.2 mile to the parking lot at the Fairway Community Center.

13 Page Meadows

A favorite hike of Tahoe locals and visitors alike, Page Meadows hosts one of the best wildflower blooms in the basin. It greens up after the snow melts, glows with color by late June, and remains a restful, scenic destination through the rest of the hiking season. A steady climb on the Tahoe Rim Trail leads to the meadows.

Start: Ward Creek Boulevard. The trail is across the road (on the north side) from the trailhead signboard and creek.
Distance: 3.2 miles out and back
Hiking time: 2–2.5 hours
Difficulty: Moderate due to length and 400-foot elevation gain
Trail surface: Singletrack and logging road
Best seasons: Late spring and early summer for the wildflower bloom
Other trail users: Mountain bikers, equestrians, off-road vehicles on adjacent trails
Trail amenities: None

Canine compatibility: Dogs permitted
Fees and permits: None
Schedule: Dawn–dusk daily
Maps: USGS Tahoe City CA; Tahoe Rim Trail map for the Barker Pass to Tahoe City section available at the trailhead and online; National Geographic 803 Lake Tahoe Basin Trail Map
Trail contact: US Forest Service Lake Tahoe Basin Management Unit, Forest Supervisor's Office, 35 College Dr., South Lake Tahoe, CA 96150; (530) 543-2600; www.fs.usda.gov/ltbmu. Tahoe Rim Trail Association, 128 Market St., Suite 3E/PO Box 3267, Stateline, NV 89449; (775) 298-4485; tahoerimtrail.org.

Finding the trailhead: From Tahoe City follow CA 89 south toward Homewood to Pineland Drive (with large "Pineland" signs). Turn right (west) onto Pineland Drive and go 0.3 mile to Twin Peaks Drive, where a sign points you toward "Ward Valley." Go left (south) onto Twin Peaks, then quickly right (west) onto Ward Creek Boulevard. Follow Ward Creek Boulevard for 1.5 miles to the signed TRT trailhead. Park alongside Ward Creek Boulevard. GPS: N39 08.435' / W120 11.522'

The Hike

High-country wildflower displays are generally modest, with clusters of flowers erupting in patches among verdant meadow grasses. The blooms of Page Meadows, situated above Ward Valley at nearly 7,000 feet, are no exception. The brilliant mule ears, with their bright-yellow sunflower-like blooms, and the tall white umbrellas of cow parsnip border on flamboyance. But most of the meadow flowers are brushed onto the landscape with a light touch. Early in the season, red Indian paintbrush, purple shooting star and lupine, scarlet larkspur, pink pussy paws, and meadow pen-stemon, among others, brighten the meadow. Later in the season, as the grasses go gold and the aspen begin to turn, white yarrow and purple and yellow asters (among others) come to the forefront.

Page Meadows, a popular destination that, luckily, is expansive enough to accommodate all comers, is surrounded by a thick evergreen forest with borders of aspens that have been sculpted into low tangles by heavy winter snowpacks. A network of trails explores the interlocking meadows; these trails are raised using cement landscaping tiles, which allow passage without damaging the ecosystem—and help to keep boots dry as well.

The section of the Tahoe Rim Trail that leads from Ward Creek to the meadows begins steeply, with the sound of Ward Creek splashing through its bed a pleasant accompani-ment. At about the 0.5-mile mark, the climb mellows; pause

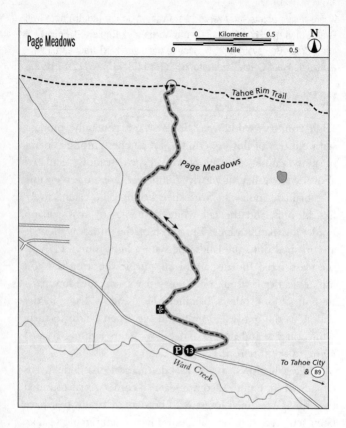

Page Meadows

Tahoe Rim Trail

Page Meadows

P 13

Ward Creek

To Tahoe City
& 89

N

to take in views of the craggy headwall of Ward Valley, where the architecture of the Granite Chief ridgetops, including Ward Peak and the backside of the Alpine Meadows ski area, is defined by snow well into June and early July.

Once on the crest, the trail is intersected by access and OHV roads, but the route is clearly marked with the distinctive TRT trail markers (white on blue), as well as other signage. Follow the winding trail through the woods until the first meadow opens before you.

A narrow raised path cuts through the thick turf of the meadow, which is wet and may be snowy early in the season, with portions underwater—shallow vernal pools—into June. Side trails branch off to explore other parts of the meadow system. The bugs can be voracious, so wear long sleeves or douse yourself in repellent—otherwise, you may not be able to linger long enough to enjoy the wildflower display.

The TRT bridges the main meadow and a smaller meadow through a narrow band of trees, then reenters the forest and rises to a sign noting the distances to the Ward Creek road and Tahoe City. This is the turnaround point. Return as you came to the trailhead.

Miles and Directions

0.0   Start on the north side of Ward Creek Boulevard. The trailhead is not obvious; look for signs marking the TRT and describing backcountry camping regulations.

0.1   At the signed junction with a steep dirt roadway, go left (west) and uphill through the woods.

0.5   The climb mellows at a bend in the road, with views west to the head of Ward Valley.

0.7   Climb to a junction marked with an OHV sign. Trail markers for the TRT, as well as a sign for Page Meadows, are about

25 yards ahead. Stay left (southwest) on the marked route, crossing two streamlets that may be dry in late season. The route narrows to singletrack.

1.1 Reach another trail junction; stay right (northwest) on the signed TRT, passing low posts that prevent motor vehicle access.

1.2 Arrive at the first meadow.

1.5 Pass through a narrow band of trees to a second, smaller meadow.

1.6 Reach a TRT trail junction with a sign noting distances to the Ward Creek road and Tahoe City. Turn around here and retrace your steps.

3.2 Arrive back at the trailhead.

14 Ellis Peak Trail

Climbing onto the ridge above Blackwood Canyon is, without question, not an easy undertaking. But the distance is short and the views from the top are a significant reward: Lake Tahoe lies broad and blue to the east, and the granite domes of the Desolation Wilderness shimmer to the west. Those with thighs of steel can continue to peaceful Ellis Lake.

Start: Signed trailhead at the summit of Barker Pass
Distance: 2.0 miles out and back
Hiking time: 1-2 hours
Difficulty: More challenging due to the 800-foot climb to the ridge
Trail surface: Rocky singletrack
Best seasons: Summer, fall
Other trail users: The occasional mountain biker
Trail amenities: None
Canine compatibility: Leashed dogs permitted
Fees and permits: None
Schedule: Sunrise–sunset daily
Maps: USGS Homewood CA; Lake Tahoe Basin Management Unit Map; National Geographic 803 Lake Tahoe Basin Trail Map; Tom Harrison Recreation Map of Lake Tahoe

Trail contact: For the trail, contact the Tahoe National Forest, 10811 Stockrest Springs Rd., Truckee, CA 96161; (530) 587-3558; www.fs.usda.gov/tahoe. For trailhead access via Barker Pass Road, contact the US Forest Service Lake Tahoe Basin Management Unit, Forest Supervisor's Office, 35 College Dr., South Lake Tahoe, CA 96150; (530) 543-2600; www.fs.usda.gov/ltbmu.
Special considerations: Given the trail's steepness and elevation gain, do not attempt if you have heart, respiratory, or knee problems. The higher elevations of Barker Pass Road receive heavy winter snow and the pass typically does not open until mid-June.

Finding the trailhead: From Tahoe City take CA 89 south for 4.1 miles to the turnoff marked for Kaspian and Blackwood Canyon. Turn right (west) onto Barker Pass Road. Stay left (south) where the road splits, crossing Blackwood Creek, and go about 7 miles to the signed trailhead on the left (west) side of the road just before the end of the pavement. Limited parking is available in pullouts along Barker Pass Road. No other amenities are available. GPS: N39 04.309' / W120 13.868'

The Hike

The splendor of the Sierran high country comes into perfect focus from a perch atop the rocky ridge crested by the Ellis Peak Trail. Cliffs drop sharply into the green valley of Blackwood Canyon, with Lake Tahoe a vast ink-blue stain on the gray and green landscape to the east. To the southwest lie the forbidding, gunmetal gray ramparts of the Desolation Wilderness, an impressive spread of flowing granite, lingering snowfields, and small, iridescent lakes.

Beyond this aerie, if you chose to go there, the mountains show another aspect of their makeup. Towering firs create a shady canopy overhead, and needles dense on the forest floor quiet the footfalls of hikers. The thunderhead-dark battlements of Ellis Peak rise above peaceful Ellis Lake, a pretty tarn in a classic alpine setting of evergreens and talus. Reaching the lake, upon consideration, is not an easy hike, but worth the effort if fitness permits.

This hike begins with a relatively brutal climb up steep switchbacks. The views begin as you climb onto a ridgetop slope where broad-leaved mule's ear and other wildflowers hunker close to the ground, out of the weather. Tortured evergreens turn barren backsides to the prevailing west wind, forming a spindly windbreak as

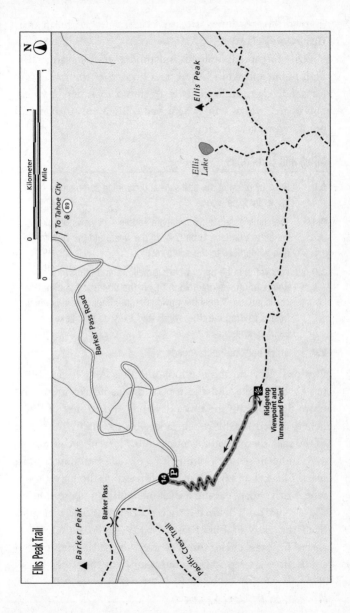

Ellis Peak Trail

N

To Tahoe City & (89)

Barker Peak

Barker Pass

Barker Pass Road

Pacific Crest Trail

14 P

Ridgetop Viewpoint and Turnaround Point

Ellis Lake

Ellis Peak

Kilometer

Mile

the route passes impressive rock outcrops that loom over Blackwood Canyon.

Uninterrupted sunlight and tundra grasses blanket the high point, and wind-lashed trees hook over the trail. Look for a side trail leading left (east) onto a rock perch, where 360-degree views can be enjoyed. This is the turnaround point; return as you came.

Miles and Directions

0.0   Start by passing the trail sign and climbing steep switch-backs into the woods.

0.4   The climb eases as you reach a saddle with views of Lake Tahoe to the east, Loon Lake to the west, and the Desolation Wilderness to the southwest.

1.0   Follow the ridge up to where it mellows and offers view-points from overlook rocks. This is the turnaround point. If you continue, follow the obvious route heading south, which begins to drop into the woods and leads to Ellis Lake and Ellis Peak.

2.0   Arrive back at the trailhead.

Options: Beyond the overlook, the Ellis Peak Trail continues to Ellis Lake and the top of the namesake mountain. From the ridgetop the route descends into a forest of thick, lichen-coated firs. Skirt a meadow on the right (west) side of the trail, then begin a gentle climb. The trail curls through a magnificent stand of old firs to a marked trail junction. To reach Ellis Lake (2.5 miles), go left (east) on the gravel four-wheel-drive road, passing a shallow pond in a depression on the left (north). The final stretch skirts a talus field that spills from the cliffs of Ellis Peak to bottle-green Ellis Lake. A mixed fir forest circles three-quarters of the lake, but on the south shore a steep spill of talus pours into the water.

To reach the summit of Ellis Peak, stay right at the signed trail junction and climb to the 8,688-foot summit. Once you've rested and refueled, return as you came. Plan on 3 to 4 hours of hiking (5–6 miles round-trip) to reach the lake and/or the peak.

You can enjoy another easy high-country ramble by traveling 0.5 mile west of the Ellis Peak trailhead on Barker Pass Road to the trailhead for the Pacific Crest Trail (PCT). A 3-mile out-and-back hike heading north on the PCT offers a sampling of the rigors and beauty of the national scenic trail. Rugged but well maintained, user-friendly but not overcrowded, this stretch of trail offers wonderful views of Blackwood Canyon, Lake Tahoe, and the Desolation Wilderness. A plug of dark volcanic rock jutting from rose-colored earth marks the end of this recommended route, though you can follow the PCT all the way to Canada if you choose.

15 General Creek Loop

Walk in the footsteps (or ski tracks) of Olympic biathletes along this woodland loop, which follows gentle General Creek into Sugar Pine Point State Park's backcountry.

Start: Day-use trailhead in the parking lot for the Sugar Pine Point State Park amphitheater
Distance: 4.7-mile lollipop
Hiking time: 3-3.5 hours
Difficulty: Moderate
Trail surface: Dirt forest roads; paved road
Best seasons: Spring, summer, fall
Other trail users: Mountain bikers, trail runners
Trail amenities: Restrooms, water, camping, and information are available in the campground.
Canine compatibility: Leashed dogs permitted on the park fire roads of this loop
Fees and permits: Day-use fee

Schedule: The Sugar Pine State Park trail system is open for year-round recreation from sunrise to sunset daily. Entrance station hours vary; in summer it is open from about 8 a.m. until 8 p.m.
Maps: USGS Homewood CA and Meeks Bay CA; map in the Sugar Pine Point State Park brochure available at the campground entrance station and online
Trail contact: Ed Z'berg Sugar Pine Point State Park, PO Box 266, Tahoma, CA 96142-0266; (530) 525-7982; www.parks. ca.gov

Finding the trailhead: From the Y junction of US 50 and CA 89 in South Lake Tahoe, follow CA 89 north for 17.5 miles to the signed entrance for Sugar Pine Point State Park. From the Y junction of CA 89 and CA 28 in Tahoe City, follow CA 89 south for 9.2 miles to the campground entrance. Proceed past the campground entrance station on the west side of the highway to parking for the campground amphitheater and the day-use trailhead. GPS (day-use trailhead): N39 03.38' / W120 07.287'

The Hike

The General Creek Loop follows part of the route biathletes traversed in the 1960 Squaw Valley Olympic Games, offering hikers a chance to gain a new appreciation for (or sense of astonishment at) one of the oddest sporting events ever conceived. In the biathlon, cross-country skiing—exhausting even when you are not racing—is paired with marksmanship; speed and accuracy determine the winner. Interpretive signs provide an introduction to the Nordic trail system established for the games, but the sign near the second bridge crossing General Creek, more than 2 miles into the woods, is the eye-opener. The pictures say it all: skiers sprawled belly-down in the snow with the rifles they've carried on their backs aimed at targets across the white meadow. Powerful imagery that's hard to grasp on a sunny summer's day.

This hike begins in the Sugar Pine Point State Park's campground. The most direct route to the trailhead proper is to follow the main campground road to the westernmost campground loop; the signed trail begins between campsites 147 and 149. A walking path skirts the campground to the south and is a nice option if you prefer to avoid pavement. An accessible campground path also leads to the westernmost camp loop.

From the camp follow the dirt fire road through a woodland cleared of underbrush. Pass a side trail that breaks left (south) into the campground, staying on the wide dirt track to the start of the loop portion of the route. Go left (south) to the first General Creek crossing; a bridge spans the

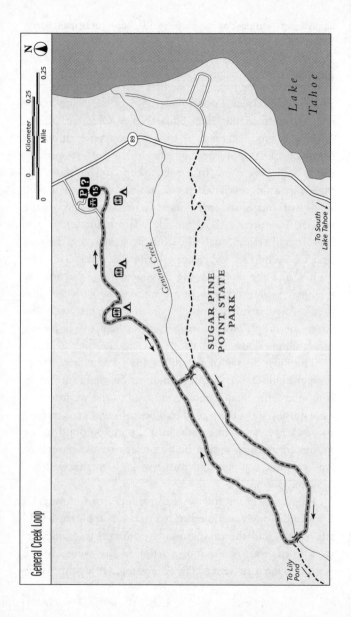

waterway. On the opposite (south) side of the creek, go right (west) on the gently climbing track.

Follow the creek westward for a meditative mile through the quiet forest and a burned area where the undergrowth is thick and lush. Bend north past the biathlon sign to the second General Creek crossing. On the north side of the bridge, the singletrack Lily Pond Trail heads left (west). Stay right on the broad General Creek Loop, which follows the north side of the creek through an old burn where wild-flowers, thimbleberries, and ferns flourish in spring and early summer.

Pass an unmarked junction with another dirt road on the descent, staying right (east). The trail/road drops to close the loop; from that point retrace your steps to the campground trailhead, then through the camp to the day-use parking lot and trail's end.

Miles and Directions

0.0   Start in the day-use/amphitheater parking lot, passing behind the closed gate on the paved roadway. Ski trail and nature trail signs mark a convergence of paved paths. Stay right on the paved trail to the main camp road, then go left (west) on the camp road. An accessible campground path also leads to the trailhead proper in the last campground loop.

0.9   Arrive at the signed General Creek trailhead, between camp-sites 147 and 149. Head down the wide graded dirt road into the woods.

1.0   Pass a side trail that leads left (south) into the campground. Stay straight on the main trail.

1.4   At the trail junction (the start of the loop) go left (south). Cross the bridge over the creek. At the trail intersection on the south bank, turn right (west).

2.4	Pass the biathlon sign and cross the creek via the bridge. The Lily Pond Trail heads left (west) on the north side of the bridge; stay right (east) on the General Creek trail.
3.1	At the unsigned junction with a dirt road, stay right (east).
3.4	Close the loop. Retrace your steps to the campground trailhead.
4.7	Arrive back at the amphitheater parking area.

Options: Sugar Pine Point offers a number of easy day hike options, including the Lakefront Interpretive Trail, the Ron Beaudry Trail, the Dolder Nature Trail, and the trail to Lily Pond. A few of the trails wind through the Edwin L. Z'berg National Preserve, named for the California state assemblyman who championed preservation and restoration efforts, and whose name was added to the park in 2004. Cap your visit to the state park with a tour of Pine Lodge (the Hellman-Ehrman mansion), an impressive 11,000-square-foot residence built as a retreat for banker Isaiah Hellman.

16 The Lighthouse and Rubicon Point

Hikers will enjoy three high points along this loop trail in D. L. Bliss State Park, and none have to do with elevation gain. The trail leads past the historic lighthouse on Rubicon Point, offers panoramic views across Lake Tahoe, and includes an exposed stretch that skims a rocky cliff above the water.

Start: Signed trailhead alongside the park road 1 mile from the entrance station

Distance: 2.5-mile loop

Hiking time: About 2 hours

Difficulty: Moderate due to elevation changes

Trail surface: Dirt singletrack; rock staircases

Best seasons: Late spring, summer, fall

Other trail users: None

Trail amenities: Restrooms, information, and picnic facilities are available in the park.

Canine compatibility: Leashed dogs permitted in the park; no dogs permitted on the trails

Fees and permits: Day-use fee

Schedule: The trail is available sunrise to sunset daily; visitor center hours vary; typically from 11 a.m. to 4 p.m. daily. If the entrance station is closed, use the self-pay registration envelopes.

Maps: USGS Emerald Bay CA; map provided in the D. L. Bliss State Park brochure

Trail contact: D. L. Bliss State Park, PO Box 266, Tahoma, CA 96142; (530) 525-7277; www.parks.ca.gov

Finding the trailhead: From the intersection of US 50 and CA 89 in South Lake Tahoe, head north on CA 89 for 12.5 miles to the signed turnoff for D. L. Bliss State Park on the right (east). From Tahoe City, take CA 89 south for 15.8 miles to the park entrance. Follow the park road 1 mile east to the trailhead, which is on the left (west) side of the road. A limited number of visitors are admitted into the park; if you arrive after 10 a.m., check at the visitor center or entrance station for availability. GPS: N38 59.353' / W120 05.915'

The Hike

The historic lighthouse that once warned sailors on Lake Tahoe of submerged dangers off Rubicon Point is unassuming—it resembles, of all the unfortunate possibilities, a wooden outhouse. But in the early days of the twentieth century, the humble structure housed a brilliant acetylene light that was integral to navigation on the lake. The light no longer steers boaters clear of the hazardous shoreline, but the lighthouse, rebuilt in 2001, makes an interesting first stop along this loop in D. L. Bliss State Park.

The lighthouse isn't the only unique man-made artifact along this route. Climbing away from Calawee Cove, the trail is etched into a steep rocky face high above the lake. A rustic railing protects the cliff side of the path, but it doesn't mitigate the thrilling exposure or impede the superlative views. *A word of caution:* This stretch is not for those afraid of heights, and children should be watched carefully.

The Lighthouse Trail begins by climbing through a fire-scarred woodland. It flattens atop a ridge amid evergreens and boulders, then drops through more hauntingly beautiful burned forest. Drop to a trail junction with great views. The granite staircase leading to the lighthouse descends steeply to the small structure perched on a rocky shelf overlooking the lake.

Climb back to the trail crossing and go right (north) on the Lighthouse Trail, which follows long, shaded switchbacks down to the paved parking area at Calawee Cove. The cove's little beach is below the lot; the signed junction with the Rubicon Trail is to the right (south). Pick up the Rubicon and head up around the namesake point.

This is the exposed stretch: The rail protects against the abrupt lakeside drop, boardwalks span clefts in the cliff face,

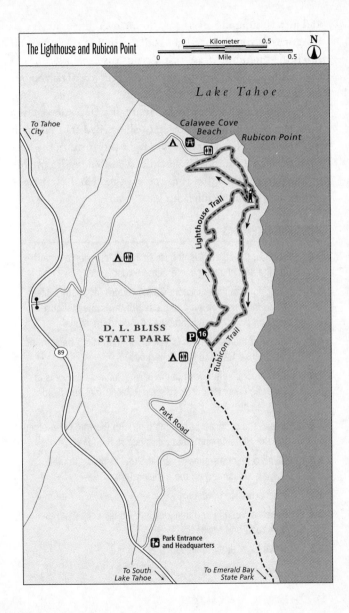

The Lighthouse and Rubicon Point

Lake Tahoe

Calawee Cove Beach

Rubicon Point

To Tahoe City

Lighthouse Trail

D. L. BLISS STATE PARK

P 16

Rubicon Trail

Park Road

89

Park Entrance and Headquarters

To South Lake Tahoe

To Emerald Bay State Park

Kilometer

Mile

N

and head-thumping overhangs loom over the trail. It's so invigorating you might forget you are climbing . . . until you reach the granite staircase that ascends past a trail leading to the lighthouse. Stay left (south) on the Rubicon Trail, enjoying heavenly views as the trail flattens.

As you near the end of the route, the trail curves away from the lake into dense forest. At the signed trail junction in a clearing, take the trail to the right (northwest); the left-hand trail leads south to Emerald Bay and Vikingsholm. The needle-carpeted path leads to the park road and the neighboring Lighthouse trailhead.

Miles and Directions

0.0   Start at the signed Lighthouse trailhead, crossing a small bridge and climbing into a burned woodland.

0.7   Drop to a trail intersection. Go left (north) for about 10 feet to an interpretive sign and the top of the stone staircase leading down to the lighthouse. Descend the stairs.

0.8   Arrive at the lighthouse. Check it out, then climb back to the Lighthouse Trail and turn right (north).

1.4   Drop through the woods to the parking lot and restrooms at Calawee Cove. Pick up the signed Rubicon Trail and head right (south).

1.6   Reach the exposed part of the trail, with the wire rail protecting the cliff side and great views across the lake.

1.8   Climb a granite staircase past the trail to the lighthouse, staying left (south) on the Rubicon Trail.

2.1   Pass a trailside overlook.

2.4   Reach a clearing and trail junction. Go right (west) to the park road and trailhead.

2.5   Arrive back at the trailhead.

17 Vikingsholm and Emerald Point

Ocean–green and opalescent, it's quite obvious how Tahoe's Emerald Bay earned its name. Spectacular Vikingsholm, at the head of the bay, is the obvious destination for most hikers. Not so obvious is the jewel of a trail that leads along the northern shoreline to the bay's narrow mouth.

Start: Emerald Bay State Park parking lot off CA 89; the signed trailhead is to the left of the huge rock slab that overlooks the bay.

Distance: 5.2 miles out and back

Hiking time: 3–4 hours

Difficulty: Moderate due to elevation change and trail length

Trail surface: Graded dirt road, pavement, and dirt singletrack

Best seasons: Spring, summer, fall

Other trail users: None

Trail amenities: A gift and information station in the parking lot; restrooms, a visitor center, and picnic facilities at Vikingsholm

Canine compatibility: Leashed dogs are permitted only in campgrounds; no dogs are permitted on trails or beaches, or at Vikingsholm and all other areas in lower Emerald Bay

Fees and permits: Parking fee

Schedule: The trail is open from sunrise to sunset. Vikingsholm and the Emerald Bay State Park visitor center are open daily from Memorial Day to Labor Day from 10 a.m. to 4 p.m., with limited hours offered earlier in May and later in Sept. Tours of Vikingsholm are available for a fee; call (530) 541-3030.

Maps: USGS Emerald Bay CA; Emerald Bay park map and brochure available online and at the visitor center

Trail contact: Emerald Bay State Park, PO Box 266, Tahoma, CA 96142; (530) 541-3030 (summer only); www.parks.ca.gov

Special considerations: The highway and parking lots at Vikingsholm and neighboring Eagle Falls are congested during high season. Lots fill quickly, with additional parking available along the roadway. Please be courteous and safe in selecting a parking space.

There is a 400-foot change in elevation within the first mile. Heed the trailhead sign that warns not to attempt the route if you have heart, respiratory, or knee problems.

Finding the trailhead: From the intersection of US 50 and CA 89 in South Lake Tahoe, head north on CA 89 for 10.7 miles to the large Emerald Bay State Park parking area on the right (southeast). From Tahoe City, take CA 89 south for 17.6 miles (parking is on the left). GPS: N38 57.261' / W120 06.619'

The Hike

Vikingsholm is arguably the most spectacular of all Lake Tahoe's shoreline estates, with striking Scandinavian architecture and views that open onto sparkling Emerald Bay. Lora Josephine Knight had the home built in 1929; she also commissioned construction of the little castle-like teahouse on the summit of Fannette Island—Lake Tahoe's only island, and, in the late 1880s, home of Captain Dick Barter, "the Hermit of Emerald Bay." The mansion, designed by architect Lennart Palme, Mrs. Knight's nephew, features huge carved timbers, massive native granite boulders mortared into exterior walls, and a sod roof sewn with wildflowers.

Hiking down to visit the storied estate is a quintessential and massively popular Tahoe excursion. But stretch a bit beyond the estate along the Rubicon Trail and you can enjoy Emerald Bay in relative solitude. Walk quietly and watchfully as you near Emerald Point; you may see an eagle or osprey return to a lakeside nest, a tangle of twigs and branches perched at the top of a standing dead tree.

Begin by heading down the wide path (a human highway in the busy summer season) to Vikingsholm. Two switchbacks separated by long traverses drop to a junction,

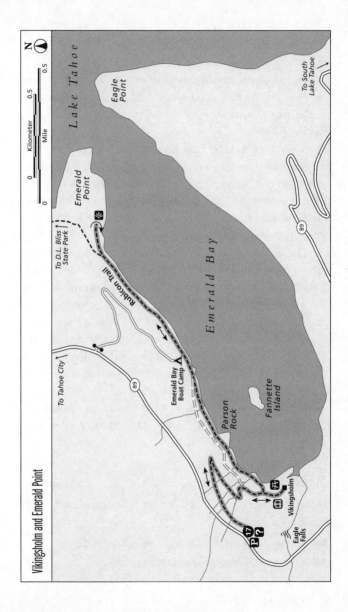

Vikingsholm and Emerald Point

where a park map points you downhill and right through open woodland to Vikingsholm. Take some time to explore the grounds, check out the visitor center, take a tour of the house, and picnic on the beach. When you're ready to move on, pick up the signed Rubicon Trail on the northeast side of the main house (the right side as you face the building from the beach).

A series of bridges and boardwalks assist passage along the forested shoreline trail, which is intersected by drainages and lush with berries, ferns, and other verdant undergrowth. It's easy going to Parson Rock, which overlooks the bay and Fannette Island just before the trail enters the Emerald Bay Boat-In Campground.

The Rubicon Trail merges with the camp road for a stretch, then breaks back to the shoreline as a dirt path at a trail sign. The easy rambling continues, with short timber stairs leading down to half-moon beaches along the waterline. The mouth of the bay, pinched by Emerald Point on the north and Eagle Point on the south, remains in sight until the Rubicon begins to bend north toward Rubicon Bay and Calawee Cove. A clearing just before the trail heads north is the turnaround point (though any of the little beaches would work just as well). Return as you came, enjoying sporadic views up into the stony Desolation Wilderness as you go.

Miles and Directions

Note: Mileages include a 0.3-mile tour of the paved paths around Vikingsholm.

0.0   Start by descending the broad, well-graded trail.

1.0   Arrive at Vikingsholm and tour the grounds.

1.3 A signed trailhead for the Rubicon Trail is to the right (north-east) of Vikingsholm as you face it. Turn right (east) onto the flat path.

1.9 Enter the Emerald Bay boat camp and follow the paved road through the campsites.

2.1 At the east end of the camp, where the pavement begins to climb, the signed Rubicon Trail breaks to the right (east), turning to dirt and following the shoreline.

2.4 Pass a series of short staircases that lead down to tiny beaches.

2.6 Reach a clearing near the tip of Emerald Point, with the obvious Rubicon Trail breaking left (north). This is the turnaround point. The social tracks dead-end in the brush. Retrace your steps back toward the trailhead.

5.2 Arrive back at the trailhead.

Option: The Rubicon Trail continues through neighboring D. L. Bliss State Park to Rubicon Point, a 4.5-mile one-way journey from Vikingsholm.

18 Eagle Lake

Dark and clear, Eagle Lake pools in a basin bordered by steep talus slopes and black-streaked rock walls. The lake's classic high Sierra setting makes it one of the most popular destinations around Lake Tahoe.

Start: Signed trailhead near the restrooms in the Eagle Falls parking lot

Distance: 2.0 miles out and back

Hiking time: About 1 hour

Difficulty: Moderate due to some steep climbing

Trail surface: Dirt singletrack, granite stairs

Best seasons: Summer, fall

Other trail users: None

Trail amenities: Restrooms, picnic sites

Canine compatibility: Leashed dogs permitted. Because the trail is so popular, owners need to keep their pets under control.

Fees and permits: Per-vehicle parking fee, if you can find space in the lot. Parking along CA 89 is free. A free wilderness permit, available at the trailhead, is required.

Schedule: Sunrise–sunset daily

Maps: USGS Emerald Bay CA; Lake Tahoe Basin Management Unit Map; National Geographic 803 Lake Tahoe Basin Trail Map; Tom Harrison's Recreation Map of Lake Tahoe

Trail contact: US Forest Service Lake Tahoe Basin Management Unit, Forest Supervisor's Office, 35 College Dr., South Lake Tahoe, CA 96150; (530) 543-2600; www.fs.usda.gov/ltbmu

Special considerations: The highway and parking lots at Eagle Falls and neighboring Vikingsholm are congested during the high season. Lots fill quickly, with additional parking available along the highway. Please be courteous and safe in selecting a parking space.

You will gain and lose about 400 feet in elevation and must climb and descend a stretch of granite steps, so be prepared for a moderate workout.

Finding the trailhead: From the intersection of US 50 and CA 89 in South Lake Tahoe, head north on CA 89 for 10.3 miles to the signed Eagle Falls parking area on the left (south). From Tahoe City follow CA 89 south for 18 miles, past the parking area for Vikingsholm, to the Eagle Falls parking lot on the right. GPS: N38 57.118' / W120 06.811'

The Hike

Eagle Lake is cupped within a stark Desolation Wilderness cirque; steep-walled, silver and gray, and formidable. The trail leading up to the lake is varied and moderately challenging but quite short, making it well within reach of any hiker seeking an alpine experience without excess effort. Though not recommended, I've even seen hikers make the ascent in strappy sandals and flip-flops.

After filling out a wilderness permit, begin by climbing the stairs behind the trailhead sign, staying on the signed Eagle Lake Trail where it connects with the shorter Eagle Loop. The path climbs gently at first, allowing you to enjoy views of the cascades above Eagle Falls, and the pinnacles and great gray domes of the Desolation Wilderness.

Nearing the cascade, a twisting stone stairway leads up, then down, to a vista point and the sturdy bridge spanning the cataract. Cross the bridge, then climb granite stairs and rocky singletrack past the wilderness boundary sign and up to a large, smooth, granite slab dotted with pine and cedar. The trail is worn into the slab; rocks line the track as well.

The trail skirts a rock outcrop overlooking the lush creek bed below, then traverses above the drainage through the woods, with the jagged crowns of the canyon walls rising above the canopy. Gentle climbing takes you to a trail

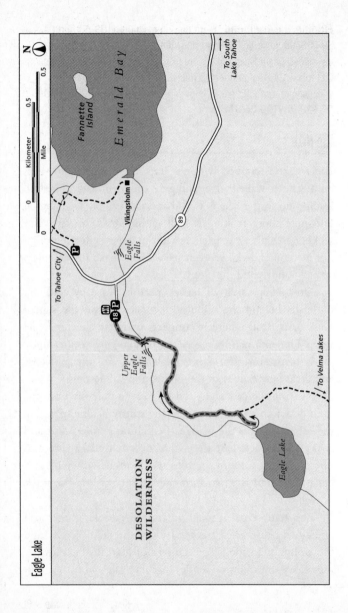

Eagle Lake

junction at 0.9 mile; from here you can head deeper into the Desolation Wilderness, to Velma Lakes and beyond. To reach Eagle Lake, however, bear right (west) into the cirque, following the arrow on the sign.

Scramble down to the shores of Eagle Lake at the 1-mile mark. A sprinkling of cedar, ponderosa, and Jeffrey pine provide shade from the vivid alpine sunshine. If you don't mind icy water, Eagle Lake invites a dip. There is no beach, however, so you'll have to dry off and/or enjoy the stunning views from a perch on a tree stump or a sunbaked granite slab.

Return the way you came, enjoying views of Lake Tahoe on the descent.

Miles and Directions

0.0   Start by climbing steps to the junction of the Eagle Lake Trail and the Eagle Loop. Stay left (southwest) on the Eagle Lake Trail.

0.2   Climb granite steps past the second Eagle Loop trail junction and stay left (south), crossing the bridge.

0.4   Pass the Desolation Wilderness boundary.

0.9   At the junction with the trail to Velma Lakes, stay right (south) on the signed trail to Eagle Lake.

1.0   Arrive at Eagle Lake. Enjoy the scenery, then retrace your steps to the trailhead.

2.0   Arrive back at the trailhead.

Options: The trail intersection just before Eagle Lake is but one gateway into the backcountry wonderland that is the Desolation Wilderness. The nearest destination is Velma Lakes, reached via a grueling climb to more than 8,000 feet, then a lovely cruise across glacier-polished granite benches through sparse forest. The Velmas are almost 5 miles from the Eagle Falls trailhead, but the wilderness offers an abundance of hiking destinations, including Dicks Lake and Fontanillis Lake, and numerous backpacking options.

19 Cascade Falls

Though the falls cascade out of sight, the views of Cascade Lake and Lake Tahoe from the smooth granite slabs at trail's end crown this moderate trek.

Start: Signed trailhead in Bayview Campground
Distance: 2.0 miles out and back
Hiking time: About 1.5 hours
Difficulty: Moderate due to climbs and descents over rocky terrain
Trail surface: Dirt and rocky singletrack; granite slabs
Best seasons: Late spring and summer, when snowmelt swells the falls
Other trail users: None
Trail amenities: Restrooms and information signboards in the campground
Canine compatibility: Leashed dogs permitted
Fees and permits: None

Schedule: Sunrise–sunset daily
Maps: USGS Emerald Bay CA; Lake Tahoe Basin Management Unit Map; National Geographic 803 Lake Tahoe Basin Trail Map; Tom Harrison Recreation Map of Lake Tahoe
Trail contact: US Forest Service Lake Tahoe Basin Management Unit, Forest Supervisor's Office, 35 College Dr., South Lake Tahoe, CA 96150; (530) 543-2600; www.fs.usda.gov/ltbmu
Other: Though the total elevation change is only about 80 feet, the trail traverses some steep, rocky terrain. Do not attempt if you have heart, respiratory, or knee problems.

Finding the trailhead: From the intersection of US 50 and CA 89 in South Lake Tahoe, head north on CA 89 for 9.4 miles to a left (south) turn into the Bayview Campground. From Tahoe City follow CA 89 south for 18.9 miles, past the parking areas for Vikingsholm and Eagle Falls, to a right turn into the campground. Follow the campground road 0.3 mile to limited parking at the signed trailhead.

Direct access to the trailhead may be difficult in high season; be prepared to park outside the campground or in safe pullouts along the
highway. GPS: N38 56.607' / W120 06.000'

The Hike

Though not in view until the end of the trail, boister-
ous Cascade Creek spills out of the high country to fuel
Cascade Falls and fill secluded Cascade Lake. The dark, still
lake, cupped in a wooded bowl and surrounded by private
property, is off-limits to hikers. The falls are off-limits too,
rendered inaccessible by steep granite faces. But above the
misting falls, hikers can chill their feet in pools and riffles as
the stream courses over and among smooth granite slabs. A
seat at trail's end on a platform of sunbaked granite affords
great vistas beyond the Cascade Lake basin to Lake Tahoe.

To begin, walk behind the information kiosk and turn
left (south) onto Cascade Trail. The trail bends around two
short trail posts in the mixed evergreen forest, then climbs a
short, stone stairway to overlook the falls, Cascade Lake, and
Lake Tahoe beyond.

At about the 0.5-mile mark, begin a rocky downward
traverse of the slope on the northwest end of Cascade Lake.
Pick your way down to and then along the base of a granite cliff, taking care, as the footing is uneven. You can catch
glimpses of the falls tumbling toward the lake, but make sure
you stop before you look.

Cross a relatively narrow ledge, then climb granite steps
and broken rock to the broad sun-splashed slabs that cradle
the creek. A lovely granite bowl opens upstream, stretching
back into Desolation Wilderness. A maze of trails has been
worked onto the landscape over the years, some marked
by "ducks" (stacks of rocks also called cairns), and others

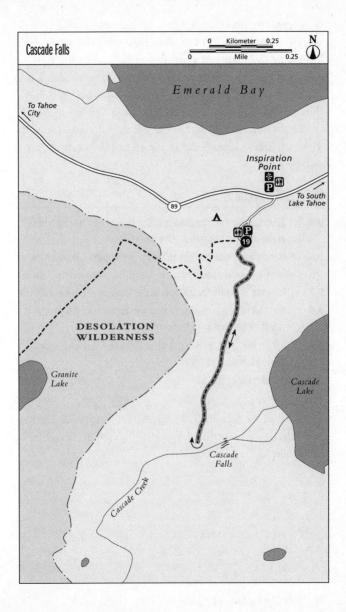

Cascade Falls

0 Kilometer 0.25
0 Mile 0.25

N

Emerald Bay

To Tahoe City

Inspiration Point

89

To South Lake Tahoe

DESOLATION WILDERNESS

Granite Lake

Cascade Lake

Cascade Falls

Cascade Creek

delineated by lines of rocks. Look left and downhill for a wooden trail marker that points the way to the falls overlook. Stay low (left and north) to get closer to the falls, but don't get too close as you don't want to take a tumble near the cliff face. Stay high (right and south) to reach stretches of the creek that permit water play and toe dipping.

The whole terrace opens on wonderful views across the southern Tahoe basin. Take in the sights, then return as you came.

Miles and Directions

0.0 Start behind the informational signboard, turning left (south) at the sign on the trail to Cascade Falls.

0.5 Head up the stone steps to views of Cascade Lake and its falls.

0.7 Traverse via slabs and steps at the base of a granite wall.

0.8 The trail levels as you approach the creek, and the granite cirque opens uphill to the south.

1.0 Reach the creek above the falls. Enjoy the sun and views, then return as you came.

2.0 Arrive back at the trailhead.

Option: A right (southwest) turn at the trailhead puts you on the trail to Granite Lake in the Desolation Wilderness. A wilderness permit for day use is required and available at the trailhead.

20 Cathedral Lake

Iconic Mount Tallac, which dominates nearly every South Lake Tahoe vista, is a powerful presence on this hike. Cathedral Lake, a peaceful tarn cupped in jumbled rock and thick-trunked evergreens, lies at the terminus of one of the 9,728-foot peak's talus fields.

Start: Mount Tallac trailhead off CA 89 near Camp Shelly
Distance: 5.6 miles out and back
Hiking time: 4–5 hours
Difficulty: More challenging due to the 1,100-foot elevation change
Trail surface: Dirt singletrack
Best seasons: Summer, early fall
Other trail users: None
Trail amenities: Information signboard
Canine compatibility: Leashed dogs permitted
Fees and permits: A free wilderness permit is required and available at the trailhead.

Schedule: 24 hours a day, 7 days a week, year-round
Maps: USGS Emerald Bay CA; Lake Tahoe Basin Management Unit Map; National Geographic 803 Lake Tahoe Basin Trail Map; Tom Harrison Recreation Map of Lake Tahoe
Trail contact: US Forest Service Lake Tahoe Basin Management Unit, Forest Supervisor's Office, 35 College Dr., South Lake Tahoe, CA 96150; (530) 543-2600; www.fs.usda.gov/ltbmu
Special considerations: Do not attempt this climb if you have heart, respiratory, or knee problems.

Finding the trailhead: From the intersection of US 50 and CA 89 in South Lake Tahoe, head north on CA 89 for 4.1 miles to the turnoff for Camp Shelly and the Mount Tallac trailhead. Turn left (west) onto the trailhead road, and drive 0.4 mile to the first fork in the road, signed for the Mount Tallac trailhead and Camp Concord. Go left (southwest) for 0.2 mile to another intersection. Stay straight (right) on FR 1306, again signed for the Mount Tallac trailhead. The parking area is 0.5 mile ahead. GPS: N38 55.283' / W120 04.086'

The Hike

The daunting rampart of Mount Tallac shadows every foot of the rustic trail to Cathedral Lake. Though the elevation gain is significant, the climbing is never painfully steep, and is mitigated by great views, shade, and a stop to rest and refuel (or turn around) at Floating Island Lake. The ultimate destination is Cathedral Lake, set in a talus-rimmed bowl near treeline on Tallac's southeast flank.

Begin by climbing the narrow track up a sunny slope covered with sage-scented scrub. Ascend a couple of switchbacks and wonderful views open of Fallen Leaf Lake below (east), and Lake Tahoe, behind and to the north.

The views improve atop the narrow ridgeback of the lateral moraine separating Fallen Leaf Lake from Mount Tallac, with the trail cruising along the spine of the moraine through Jeffrey pine and mountain hemlock. Drop off the ridge into a drainage, where the views are abandoned for shade.

The trail roller-coasters through forest and gully as it veers north into the shadow of the mountain. Climb up to and then alongside the creek that issues from Floating Island Lake. Enter the Desolation Wilderness, then hitch up a final stretch to the flat, quiet shoreline of the little lake.

The trail skirts the forested south shore of Floating Island Lake. At the edge of a small talus field just above the lake, the trail veers right (west), resuming the climb via a short staircase composed of blocks of granite. Cross a small meadow and a creek (stay left on the main trail); beyond, the route traverses a hillside strewn with wildflowers and butterflies in early summer.

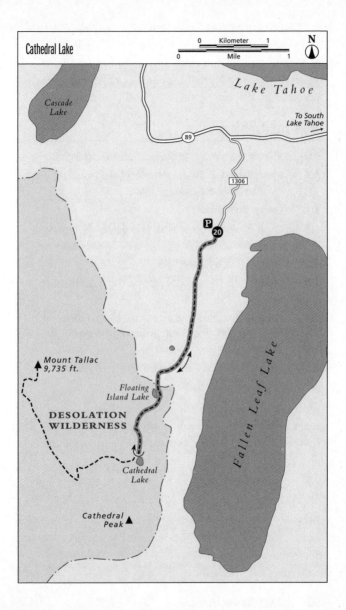

Cathedral Lake

0 Kilometer 1
0 Mile 1

N

Lake Tahoe

Cascade
Lake

To South
Lake Tahoe

89

1306

P
20

Mount Tallac
9,735 ft.

Floating
Island Lake

DESOLATION
WILDERNESS

Fallen Leaf Lake

Cathedral
Lake

Cathedral
Peak

Drop to a second creek crossing, then meander up to the junction with a trail that descends to Fallen Leaf Lake. Stay right (southwest), climbing a last pitch up to Cathedral Lake. Rest on the shores of the small tarn, then return to the trailhead by the same route.

Miles and Directions

0.0   Start up the trail behind the informational signboard.

0.7   Reach the top of the lateral moraine, and take in the views of Fallen Leaf Lake and Lake Tahoe.

1.2   Drop off the moraine.

1.8   Climb up along a creek to the boundary of the Desolation Wilderness.

1.9   Arrive at Floating Island Lake.

2.5   Cross a streamlet and stay right (west) around the talus field.

2.7   Arrive at the signed junction with the trail to Fallen Leaf Lake. Stay right (southwest) and up on the Mount Tallac Trail.

2.8   Arrive at Cathedral Lake. Rest, then retrace your steps.

5.6   Arrive back at the trailhead.

Options: If you've the will and strength, you can make the steep climb to the summit of Mount Tallac, a hiker's prize reached about 2.4 miles above and beyond Cathedral Lake.

21 Rainbow Trail

The Taylor Creek Stream Profile Chamber is the main attraction along this charming and popular paved path, but there's more to recommend the Rainbow Trail, including vistas across the marsh surrounding Taylor Creek, bowers of quaking aspen, and comprehensive interpretive signage.

Start: Opposite the Taylor Creek Visitor Center near the Tallac Historic Site, marked with an arch
Distance: 0.6-mile loop
Hiking time: About 45 minutes
Difficulty: Easy
Trail surface: Pavement
Best seasons: Spring, summer, fall
Other trail users: None
Trail amenities: Restrooms, information, water, visitor center
Canine compatibility: Dogs not permitted in the stream chamber or on Kiva Beach, but otherwise allowed on leashes
Fees and permits: None
Schedule: The Taylor Creek Stream Profile Chamber is open Memorial Day to Oct 31 from 8

a.m. until a half hour before the Taylor Creek Visitor Center closes. The Taylor Creek Visitor Center's operating hours vary, but it is generally open from 8 a.m. to 4:30 p.m. from mid-May to mid-June and during Oct, and from 8 a.m. to 5:30 p.m. from mid-June through Sept. The trails can be used from sunrise to sunset daily.
Maps: USGS Emerald Bay CA, but a map is not needed
Trail contact: US Forest Service Lake Tahoe Basin Management Unit, Forest Supervisor's Office, 35 College Dr., South Lake Tahoe, CA 96150; (530) 543-2600; www.fs.usda.gov/ltbmu
Special considerations: The trail is wheelchair accessible.

Finding the trailhead: From the intersection of US 50 and CA 89 in South Lake Tahoe, go northwest on CA 89 for 3.2 miles to the signed turnoff for the Taylor Creek Visitor Center. Turn right (north)

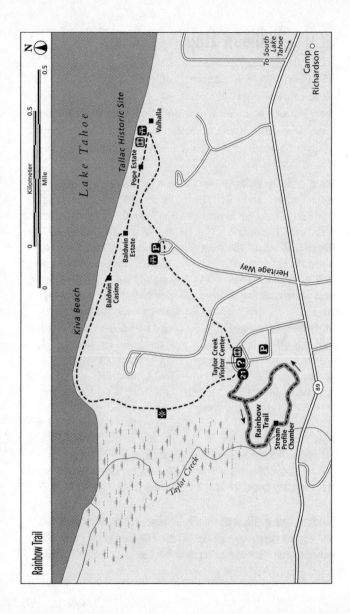

Rainbow Trail

onto the visitor center road, and follow it to the parking area. GPS: N38 56.133' / W120 03.243'

The Hike

In the clear water behind the glass of the Taylor Creek Stream Profile Chamber, kokanee salmon, their scales lipstick red as they prepare to spawn in autumn, seem to pace in lovesick agitation. They mingle with their cousins: rainbow, brown, and Lahontan cutthroat trout, the latter species native to the deep waters of Lake Tahoe. Larger fish circle lazily in the stream while the smaller dart about swiftly, looking for food or perhaps hoping to avoid becoming a meal themselves.

This opportunity to observe life inside a mountain stream from fish-eye level is the highlight of the Rainbow Trail, the experience enhanced by the assistance of a naturalist and information presented on the surrounding interpretive display. But this pleasant walk—easy enough for a toddler to manage—sports many other attractions. The marsh surrounding Taylor Creek is no scenic slouch, resplendent with wildflowers in spring and ringing with birdcall throughout the hiking season. Quaking aspen, turning as vivid a gold as the kokanee's red in fall, provide yet another visual lollipop. The route is lined with interpretive signs and benches, perfect for the entertainment and edification of children of all ages.

The path begins just outside the visitor center, dropping to a marsh overlook and then to a trail junction where the loop begins. Go right (following the arrow), traveling in a counterclockwise direction. Meander through the meadow and skirt the marsh on boardwalks, pausing to take in views toward Lake Tahoe and read the interpretive signs. A bridge spans Taylor Creek, then the trail forks, with one branch leading down and through the stream profile chamber and the other going around. Head down the path into the chamber, view the trout action, then climb back out onto the paved path.

On the far side of the chamber, amid the aspen, pass a "pillow sensor" and rain gauge, along with an interpretive display that explains their functions. Beyond lies an alder spring, and then the tall grasses and wildflowers of the meadow accompany you back to the trail fork. Go right to the visitor center and parking area.

Miles and Directions

0.0   Start on the paved path under the Rainbow Trail arch.

0.1   Visit the marsh overlook, then return to the trail and drop to the start of the loop. Go right (counterclockwise) as indicated by the arrow on the small sign.

0.3   Drop through the stream profile chamber.

0.4   At the Y outside the chamber, go left, past the monitoring station. Close the loop by circling back toward the visitor center.

0.6   Arrive back at the trailhead.

22 Lake of the Sky Trail and Tallac Historic Site

Lake Tahoe's natural history is juxtaposed with its human history on this pleasant meander, which begins with an exploration of the Taylor Creek Marsh and ends among the spectacular vacation homes of turn-of-the-twentieth-century tycoons.

Start: North side of the Taylor Creek Visitor Center on the signed Lake of the Sky Trail

Distance: 2.0-mile loop

Hiking time: About 1 hour

Difficulty: Easy

Trail surface: Dirt trail, sand, and pavement

Best seasons: Late spring, summer, fall

Other trail users: Cyclists, trail runners

Trail amenities: Restrooms, information, water, visitor center

Canine compatibility: No dogs permitted on the portion of Kiva Beach west of Kiva Point. Leashed dogs are allowed on the section of beach that is part of the Kiva Picnic Area. Though leashed dogs are allowed on the trails, Tallac Historic Site is not dog friendly.

Fees and permits: None

Schedule: The Taylor Creek Visitor Center's operating hours vary, but it is generally open from 8 a.m. to 4:30 p.m. from mid-May to mid-June and during Oct, and from 8 a.m. to 5:30 p.m. from mid-June through Sept. The trails can be used from sunrise to sunset daily.

Maps: USGS Emerald Bay CA; Lake Tahoe Basin Management Unit Map; National Geographic 803 Lake Tahoe Basin Trail Map; Tom Harrison Recreation Map of Lake Tahoe

Trail contact: US Forest Service Lake Tahoe Basin Management Unit, Forest Supervisor's Office, 35 College Dr., South Lake Tahoe, CA 96150; (530) 543-2600; www.fs.usda.gov/ltbmu

Other: The beach walk from the end of Lake of the Sky Trail to the Tallac Historic Site is not a formal forest service trail.

Finding the trailhead: From the intersection of US 50 and CA 89 in South Lake Tahoe, go northwest on CA 89 for 3.2 miles to the signed turnoff for the Taylor Creek Visitor Center. Turn right (north) onto the visitor center road, and follow it to the parking area for the visitor center. GPS: N38 56.165' / W120 03.228'

The Hike

Lake Tahoe has proven itself the perfect habitat for a variety of residents, from the Washoe Indians who summered in the basin to turn-of-the-twentieth-century vacationers who built grand estates and party palaces on its shoreline . . . not to mention the wild creatures—deer, eagles, bear, and trout, to name a few—that have called the lake home for thousands of years. This trail loop offers glimpses into what each found here, and what they left behind.

The tour begins on the Lake of the Sky Trail, which heads north from the Taylor Creek Visitor Center, paralleling the Taylor Creek Marsh to Kiva Beach at Tallac Point. The trail is lined with interpretive signs and boasts a viewing deck overlooking the marsh.

At Kiva Beach the formal trail ends, and an informal trail leads east along the beach toward the Tallac Historic Site. Wander down along the waterside for a stretch—you'll likely see boats pulling water-skiers and wakeboarders—then hitch right (south) up one of the short staircases onto the doubletrack at the interface between forest and beach. Pass the foundations of the Tallac Resort Casino; an interpretive sign describes the ballroom, gambling rooms, bowling alley, and stage that "Lucky" Baldwin built and operated on the site. Baldwin's purchase of the lakefront property in 1880 also resulted in the preservation of the grand old Jeffrey pines that shade picnic areas along the trail.

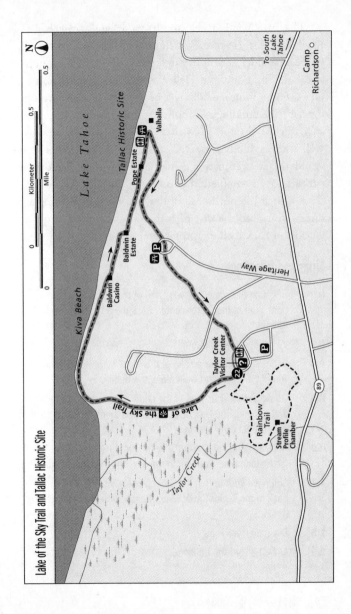

Lake of the Sky Trail and Tallac Historic Site

The path bends right (south) to a gate at the edge of the Tallac Historic Site. Pass through: Once within the site, you can wander at will through the grounds of the impressive Baldwin, Pope, and Heller estates. The exploration can take a few minutes, or the rest of the day. Interpretive signs describe the buildings—cabins, impressive lodges, a museum, a boathouse theater, all with tree-screened lake views—as well as the exhibits preserved at the site. Be sure to visit the wonderful arboretum and garden before you head out to the parking lot to complete the loop.

A sign at the north end of the historic site's parking area directs you onto the dirt path that leads through scrub and woodland back to the visitor center and trailhead.

Miles and Directions

0.0   Begin on the signed, paved Lake of the Sky Trail on the north side of the visitor center. Pass the amphitheater; the trail turns to dirt.

0.2   Visit the viewing platform.

0.4   Reach the end of the Lake of the Sky Trail at Kiva Beach. Turn right (east) and walk along the beach.

0.6   Go right (south) up one of the short staircases onto the trail that parallels the beach. Go left (east) along the wide track past the Baldwin casino.

0.9   The trail bends right (south) to the first buildings of the Tallac Historic Site. Go left into the site, then wander at will.

1.7   Complete your tour in the main parking lot. The signed path back to the Taylor Creek Visitor Center is on the north side of the lot.

1.8   Cross the park road.

2.0   Arrive back at the trailhead.

23 Lam Watah Nature Trail

Follow trail and boardwalk through meadows and stands of Jeffrey pine from Stateline's busy casino district to Lake Tahoe's sprawling Nevada Beach.

Start: Signed trailhead at the junction of US 50 and Kahle Drive
Distance: 2.3 miles out and back
Hiking time: About 1.5 hours
Difficulty: Easy
Trail surface: Decomposed granite, boardwalk, asphalt, and sand
Best seasons: Spring, summer, fall
Other trail users: Mountain bikers, trail runners
Trail amenities: Restrooms and information signboards; camping and picnic sites at Nevada Beach

Canine compatibility: Leashed dogs permitted on trail; no dogs allowed on Nevada Beach
Fees and permits: None
Schedule: Sunrise–sunset daily
Maps: USGS South Lake Tahoe (CV, NV); National Geographic 803 Lake Tahoe Basin Trail Map
Trail contact: US Forest Service Lake Tahoe Basin Management Unit, Forest Supervisor's Office, 35 College Dr., South Lake Tahoe, CA 96150; (530) 543-2600; www.fs.usda.gov/ltbmu

Finding the trailhead: The trailhead is just northeast of Stateline's casino district at the corner of US 50 and Kahle Drive. Turn left (north) onto Kahle Drive, then immediately right into the signed parking lot. GPS: N38 58.251' / W119 56.151'

The Hike

Linking the busy casinos of Stateline with Tahoe's shoreline at Nevada Beach, the Lam Watah Trail traverses swatches of meadow and open pine woodland, a wide and gentle walk-and-talk route perfect for a sunset stroll or a short family hike.

Though the route never wanders far from civilization—houses are visible along Kahle Road at the outset and the towers of the casinos and the Heavenly Valley gondola rise against the mountain front on the return—the essence of the trail is in the woods and the meadows. Wildflowers light the grasses in spring, and the trees provide shade and a distinctive windblown song played only in the high country. A variety of birds settle in the brush along the willow-bordered stream and pond near the trailhead, and at the end Lake Tahoe spreads northward as far as the eye can see.

The pond is to the right (north) as the trail begins its gentle descent toward the beach. Social trails cut right to the pond and left toward the homes through high desert sages; stay straight on the obvious path. A copse of aspen at the edge of the pond is a bird magnet.

Cross the stream below the pond via a curving boardwalk, then enter the first patch of woodland. From here to the beachside campground, the well-composed trail drops through meadows and rises through the woods in gentle undulations. Benches are placed along the track for rest and contemplation. In the distance the craggy peaks of the Desolation Wilderness cut the horizon.

The route ends at a signed trailhead in the Nevada Beach Campground. To reach the beach, follow the campground road around to the right (north, then southwest) to sandy access trails near the restrooms. Dogs are not allowed on the beach, but it is the perfect place to cool your feet before retracing your steps to the trailhead.

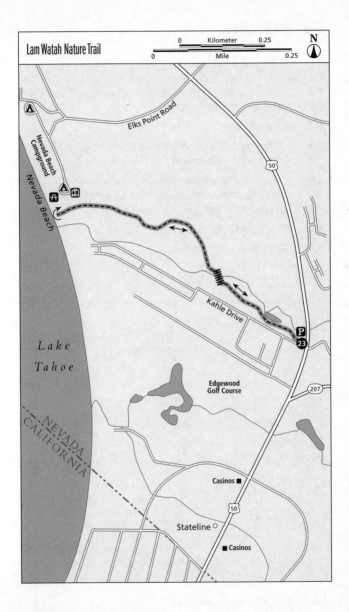

Lam Watah Nature Trail

Kilometer
0   0.25

Mile
0   0.25

N

Elks Point Road

Nevada Beach Campground

Nevada Beach

50

Kahle Drive

P
23

Lake Tahoe

Edgewood Golf Course

NEVADA
CALIFORNIA

207

Casinos ■

Stateline ○

■ Casinos

50

Miles and Directions

0.0 Start by heading down the wide gravel track toward Lake Tahoe.

0.1 Pass the pond. Ignore social trails that break right and left, staying on the main track.

0.3 Cross the boardwalk.

0.4 Trails merge in the woods; remain on the main track heading west toward the lakeshore.

1.0 Arrive at the Lam Watah trailhead in the campground. Follow the campground road around to the right (north), then left (southwest) to the sandy beach access by the restrooms.

1.1 Reach the beach, relax a while, then retrace your steps.

2.3 Arrive back at the trailhead.

24 Angora Lakes

Throw the suits and towels into the day pack and bring the kids: The Angora Lakes Trail is short, sweet, and lovely—the perfect introduction to the pleasures of hiking in the mountains around Lake Tahoe.

Start: Signed trailhead beyond the gate at the south end of the upper parking lot
Distance: 1.0 mile out and back
Hiking time: About 45 minutes
Difficulty: Easy
Trail surface: Dirt access road
Best seasons: Summer, fall
Other trail users: Mountain bikers and the occasional automobile
Trail amenities: Restrooms, fee stations, and an information sign are in the trailhead parking lot. Boat rentals, swimming, gifts, food, and fresh lemonade are available at the Angora Lakes Resort.
Canine compatibility: Leashed dogs permitted; dogs may not swim in the lake

Fees and permits: Parking fee
Schedule: Hike the trail from sunrise to sunset daily. The resort is open daily from mid-June to mid-Sept.
Maps: USGS Echo Lakes CA, but no map is necessary
Trail contact: US Forest Service Lake Tahoe Basin Management Unit, Forest Supervisor's Office, 35 College Dr., South Lake Tahoe, CA 96150; (530) 543-2600; www.fs.usda.gov/ltbmu
Other: Angora Lakes Resort offers day users access to the snack shack (where the lemonade is sold) and kayak and boat rentals. Cabins book well in advance; visit angoralakesresort. com or call (530) 541-2092 for more information.

Finding the trailhead: From the intersection of US 50 and CA 89 in South Lake Tahoe, go northwest on CA 89 for 3 miles to Fallen Leaf Lake Road. Turn left (west) onto Fallen Leaf Lake Road and go 2 miles to Tahoe Mountain Road. Turn left (southwest) onto Tahoe

Mountain Road and follow it for 0.4 mile to unsigned FR 1214 (look for an open gate; the road appears to be dirt at the outset). Turn right (west) onto FR 1214 and travel 3 miles on the scenic, narrow, paved roadway to the parking area. GPS: N38 52.261' / W120 03.788'

The Hike

A short romp up the Angora Lakes Resort access road, with just enough elevation gain to get your heart pumping, leads to the sandy shoreline of Upper Angora Lake. The setting is postcard-perfect, with the blue-green lake pooling in a basin at the base of the stark gray-and-black rock faces of Echo and Angora Peaks. Trail's end brings cool water for swimming, rowboats for rent, and a snack bar that features some of the best lemonade money can buy. It's not a wilderness experience, but the short hike leads to one of the South Shore's most desirable destinations.

Begin by following the access road as it loops in broad arcing turns up a boulder-strewn, forested hillside. After the short climb, the path flattens and is intersected by social paths that lead right (south) to private cabins on Lower Angora Lake. Stay left (southwest) on the main track, tracing the north shore of the lower lake.

An exceptionally brief climb leads to the snack bar and cabins on the eastern shores of Upper Angora Lake. The west and north shores are contained by black-streaked terraced cliffs spilling down from Echo and Angora Peaks. The beach hugs the north shore: Stake out a patch of sand, sip some luscious fresh-squeezed lemonade, and enjoy.

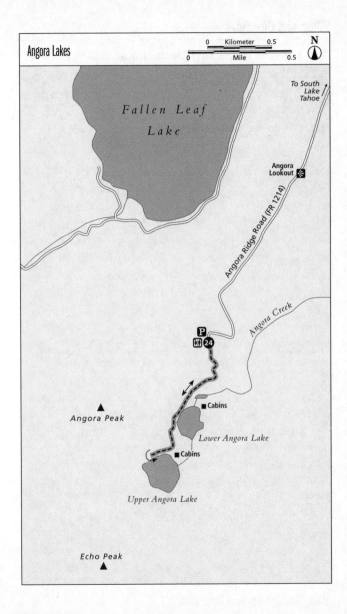

Angora Lakes

0 Kilometer 0.5
0 Mile 0.5

N

To South Lake Tahoe

Fallen Leaf Lake

Angora Lookout

Angora Ridge Road (FR 1214)

Angora Creek

P 🚻 24

Angora Peak ▲

Cabins ■

Lower Angora Lake

Cabins ■

Upper Angora Lake

Echo Peak ▲

Miles and Directions

0.0   Start by heading up on the broad, busy dirt track.

0.2   Reach Lower Angora Lake.

0.5   Rest on the shores of Upper Angora Lake, then retrace your steps.

1.0   Arrive back at the trailhead.

25 Glen Alpine

Though the native Washoe were the first to enjoy the springs at what would become known as Glen Alpine Springs Resort, it was Nathan Gilmore, prospector and cofounder of the Sierra Club, who would turn the area into Lake Tahoe's first bona fide upscale getaway. This easy walk up a forest road paved in river stones leads to the remnants of the resort.

Start: Gated Glen Alpine trailhead at Lily Lake

Distance: 2.2 miles out and back

Hiking time: About 1.5 hours

Difficulty: Easy

Trail surface: River stone and dirt roadway

Best seasons: Late spring, summer, fall

Other trail users: None

Trail amenities: Parking, restrooms, information signboard, trash cans at the trailhead; information signboards at the Glen Alpine resort site

Canine compatibility: Leashed dogs permitted

Fees and permits: A free wilderness permit is required if you decide to proceed into Desolation Wilderness, which begins just beyond the Glen Alpine site. The permit is available at the trailhead.

Schedule: 24 hours a day, 7 days a week, year-round

Maps: USGS Emerald Bay CA; Lake Tahoe Basin Management Unit Map; National Geographic 803 Lake Tahoe Basin Trail Map; Tom Harrison Recreation Map of Lake Tahoe

Trail contact: US Forest Service Lake Tahoe Basin Management Unit, Forest Supervisor's Office, 35 College Dr., South Lake Tahoe, CA 96150; (530) 543-2600; www.fs.usda.gov/ltbmu

Special considerations: Parking is limited at the Glen Alpine trailhead, though improvements/expansion are in the works. More parking is available in pullouts along the access road. Fallen Leaf Lake Road is one lane and busy in summer. Travel slowly and be courteous by stopping in wide spots to let oncoming traffic pass safely.

Finding the trailhead: From the intersection of US 50 and CA 89 in South Lake Tahoe, go north on CA 89 for 3 miles to Fallen Leaf Lake Road. Turn left (west) onto Fallen Leaf Lake Road. Pass the turnoff for Angora Lakes at about 2 miles, continuing on Fallen Leaf Lake Road for a total of 5 miles. Pass the lodge and marina, and at the fork just beyond, stay straight, past the fire station, on FR 1216 to Lily Lake. The trailhead parking area is 0.6 mile ahead. GPS: N38 52.627' / W120 04.836'

The Hike

If a hard line could be drawn in the woods, there would be one just above the site of the historic Glen Alpine Springs Resort. Where the gravel road ends and the trail begins, the personality of the backcountry changes abruptly. Below the granite staircase, remnants of civilization, including a burbling spring and the historic structures of a nineteenth-century resort, huddle on granite slopes among the pines. Step onto the staircase and you've left civilization behind: You are in the wilderness.

As with most trails in the Tahoe basin, the Glen Alpine changes with the seasons. In early season or during heavy snow years, the route may be half submerged in flowing snowmelt. The stretch from Lily Lake to the Glen Alpine resort site can be soggy, but the pair of waterfalls spilling down the creek adjacent to the road are invigorating and entertaining.

At the outset, the trail is an access road surfaced in ankle-twisting cobbles. Gates and trail signs keep you on track at forks in the road, though the signs are inconspicuous— brown and mounted above eye level on tree trunks. Parcels of private land line this section of the route, with rugged driveways leading to small cabins.

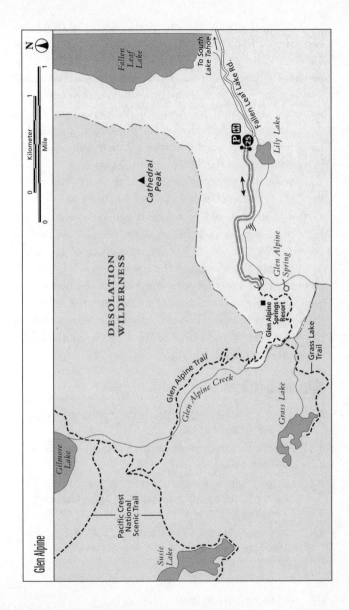

Glen Alpine

Patches of asphalt are interspersed with the cobbles as you approach the first series of cascades on Glen Alpine Creek at 0.4 mile, the largest of which is about 30 feet in height. The display is best (and loudest) in June and early July. Past the falls the trail climbs to another driveway intersection; go left (west), following the trail sign.

Continue past several more cabins, traveling through a lovely mixed evergreen forest with a lush understory of wild berries and flowers that bloom in spring, and deciduous trees and shrubs that turn yellow and orange in fall. The cabins have all of the Desolation Wilderness as a backyard.

Just beyond an old barn, a trail sign points you to the right (west) and into what is left of the Glen Alpine Springs Resort, which operated for the better part of a century. Take a break and check out the ruins of the once-thriving enterprise, including the soda spring, which still burbles and pops. Interpretive signs thoroughly describe the history of the resort, and a map directs you to the different structures that were part of the complex. After you've finished your exploration, return as you came.

Miles and Directions

0.0   Start by passing the green gate at the trailhead and walking up the cobbled roadway.

0.3   Cross a stream (dry in late season) and pass a gate and trail sign.

0.4   At the junction with a private access road, stay right and follow the "Trails" sign. Check out the Glen Alpine falls before continuing up the riverstone roadway.

0.5   At a second junction with a private drive, stay left, again following the "Trails" sign.

1.1   Pass the old barn and enter the Glen Alpine Springs Resort. Explore the site, then return as you came.

2.2   Arrive back at the trailhead.

Options: A number of enticing destinations lie above the Glen Alpine resort site in the Desolation Wilderness. With two lakes, two waterfalls, and three creek crossings, the hike to Grass Lake is invigorating if not exactly easy. The junction with the trail leading to the little lake is 1.8 miles from the trailhead (0.7 mile past Glen Alpine). You'll have to negotiate a triplet of creek crossings to reach the lake basin, which could be tricky in early season when runoff is at its height. The lake is at 2.5 miles, cupped in a glacial basin with a seasonal waterfall spilling down the opposite cliff in early season.

If you continue on the Glen Alpine Trail past the Grass Lake turnoff, you will climb deeper into Desolation. Gilmore Lake lies 4.3 miles from the trailhead, in a shallow bowl on the slopes of Mount Tallac. And Tallac itself is a goal, albeit out of the easy range, with the summit at more than 9,700 feet. Other destinations include Susie Lake, Half Moon Lake, and Lake Aloha, all of which are worthy of an overnight trip as much as an arduous day hike.

26 Pacific Crest Trail at Echo Lakes

This leg of the famous Pacific Crest Trail stretches from the exposed granite slabs that border Lower Echo Lake to the forested shore of the Upper Echo Lake. The hiking is easy and the views arc north into the craggy silver heights of the Desolation Wilderness.

Start: Signed Pacific Crest Trail (PCT)/Tahoe Rim Trail (TRT) trailhead on the far side of the dam behind Echo Chalet

Distance: 2.5 miles one-way (with a boat taxi shuttle) or 5.0 miles out and back

Hiking time: 1–2 hours one-way or 3–4 hours out and back

Difficulty: Moderate due to trail length and rocky terrain

Trail surface: Dirt and rock singletrack

Best seasons: Summer, fall

Other trail users: None

Trail amenities: Food, lodging, restrooms, and information are available at the trailhead. A dock and direct telephone line to the boat taxi are at the Upper Echo Lake endpoint; there is also a credit card–only pay phone.

Canine compatibility: Leashed dogs permitted

Fees and permits: There is no fee if you hike out and back; a fee is charged for the on-demand boat taxi. You must fill out a free permit, available at the trailhead, if you plan to hike into the Desolation Wilderness.

Schedule: The trail can be hiked sunrise to sunset daily. Boat taxis are available until 5:30 p.m. in the summer months.

Maps: USGS Echo Lakes CA; National Geographic 803 Lake Tahoe Basin Trail Map; Tom Harrison Recreation Map of Lake Tahoe

Trail contact: US Forest Service Lake Tahoe Basin Management Unit, Forest Supervisor's Office, 35 College Dr., South Lake Tahoe, CA 96150; (530) 543-2600; www.fs.usda.gov/ltbmu. Tahoe Rim Trail Association, 128 Market St., Suite 3E/PO Box 3267, Stateline, NV 89449; (775) 298-4485; tahoerimtrail.org

Finding the trailhead: From the junction of US 50 and CA 89 in South Lake Tahoe, drive west on US 50 for 10 miles, over Echo Summit, to a right (north) turn onto Johnson Pass Road (with sign). Go 0.5 mile on Johnson Pass Road to Echo Lakes Road. Turn left (north) onto Echo Lakes Road and drive 1.2 miles to the Echo Chalet. Parking can be tight; if no parking is available at the chalet, scout a spot along the road or in the upper parking lot, and walk the short distance down to the chalet and trailhead. Contact the Forest Service for latest parking options and restrictions. GPS: N38 50.085' / W120 02.611'

The Hike

The granite basin that holds the Echo Lakes, at the edge of the Desolation Wilderness and near the crest of the Sierra, provides a lovely setting for this stretch of the combined Pacific Crest Trail (PCT) and Tahoe Rim Trail (TRT). The lower lake is larger and the route is exposed to the sun and wind, with the granite base of Flagpole Peak underlying the treadway. To the north, the broad pass between Keiths Dome (on the northwest side) and Ralston Peak (on the southwest side) forms a headwall of great silvery terraces, a beckoning and imposing gateway into the wilderness beyond. The upper lake, by contrast, is screened from hikers' view by the dense pine and fir forest that crowds its shoreline; the trail here is enveloped in peaceful green.

The hike begins at the southern end of the lower lake near the Echo Chalet. Cross the causeway atop the dam and the bridge that spans the spillway. The trail switches uphill past trail signs to a trail intersection; head left (north) on Pacific Crest Trail, climbing up through manzanita onto granite slabs. The trail is etched in the bleached granite, a narrow but well-traveled traverse that stays about 200 feet above the surface of the navy-blue water.

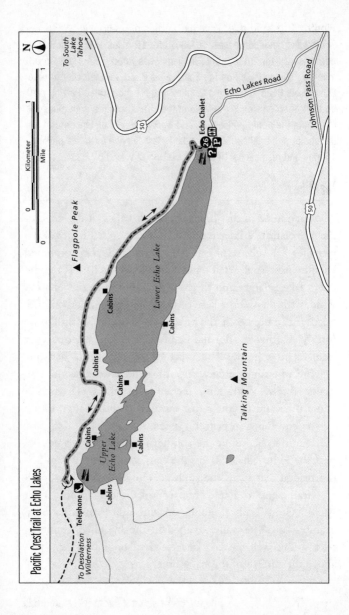
Pacific Crest Trail at Echo Lakes

N

To South Lake Tahoe

Flagpole Peak

To Desolation Wilderness

Telephone

Upper Echo Lake

Cabins

Cabins

Cabins

Cabins

Cabins

Cabins

Lower Echo Lake

Talking Mountain

Echo Chalet

Echo Lakes Road

Johnson Pass Road

Kilometer

Mile

Not far beyond a section of trail that has been augmented with asphalt, pass above the first of many charming vacation cabins that line both lakes. Gentle climbing leads to a trail sign near some of those cabins, then two switchbacks lead up the steepest part of the hike, with the ascent moderating again as you approach the far reaches of the lower lake.

The route drops through a rocky, brushy section in the shadow of an overhanging slab streaked with black, gray, and orange. Climb through the gap between the two lakes, where the trail and bordering hillside are stained orange with iron that has oxidized in the rock. The trail bends back to the north, offering brief views of the upper lake and the stony islands of the narrow passage between the two blue tarns.

The easy traverse along the wooded shores of the upper lake offers no views, but the forest shades a colorful understory of brush and wildflowers that rings with birdcall. Crest a small rise; as you begin to head downhill, look for the "Taxi" sign nailed to a big fir tree. The narrow path to the boat dock branches off to the left (west) from this point. Drop about 50 yards to the dock, which is the turnaround point. You can either take a break on the dock overlooking the upper lake, then hike back as you came, or pick up the phone and call for the boat taxi. I recommend the taxi: The ride across both lakes is a treat.

Miles and Directions

0.0   Start by crossing the dam at the south end of Lower Echo Lake. At the Tahoe Rim Trail/Pacific Crest Trail signs and map, head up and right, then around left (north) to parallel the lakeshore.

0.3   Climb across a granite slab.

1.1 Pass a trail sign above a cluster of cabins. The trail switch-backs up the hillside.

1.6 Pass a black-streaked overhanging rock on the right, then the trail flattens alongside cabins.

2.0 Cross the red soils of the isthmus separating the upper and lower lakes.

2.3 Pass through an open woodland filled with wildflowers and birdsong.

2.5 At the "Taxi" sign nailed onto a tree, turn left (west) and drop to the boat dock. This is the turnaround point for an out-and-back hike or the place to call for the boat taxi.

5.0 Arrive back at the trailhead.

Options: The PCT and TRT continue into Desolation Wilderness, a high-country wonderland of lakes. The wilderness is a backpacker's paradise; you can do a long loop, then return to Upper Echo Lake to take a taxi back to your car.

27 Big Meadow

A quick climb along a churning creek leads to the seductive expanse of Big Meadow, alive with wildflowers that change color with the seasons. The waterway becomes a meander among the grasses, where you are likely to find yourself alone with its chatter and the wind rustling the pines.

Start: Lower parking lot at the Big Meadow trailhead on CA 89

Distance: 2.0 miles out and back

Hiking time: About 1 hour

Difficulty: Easy

Trail surface: Dirt singletrack

Best seasons: Late spring, summer, fall

Other trail users: Mountain bikers, equestrians

Trail amenities: Restrooms, trash cans, and an information signboard with map at the trailhead

Canine compatibility: Leashed dogs permitted

Fees and permits: None

Schedule: Sunrise–sunset daily

Maps: USGS Freel Peak and Echo Lake CA; National Geographic 803 Lake Tahoe Basin Trail Map; Tahoe Rim Trail map available at the trailhead

Trail contact: US Forest Service Lake Tahoe Basin Management Unit, Forest Supervisor's Office, 35 College Dr, South Lake Tahoe, CA 96150; (530) 543-2600; www.fs.usda.gov/ltbmu. Tahoe Rim Trail Association, 128 Market St., Suite 3E/PO Box 3267, Stateline, NV 89449; (775) 298-4485; tahoerimtrail.org.

Finding the trailhead: From the intersection of US 50 and CA 89 in South Lake Tahoe, drive south on US 50/CA 89 for 4.7 miles to Meyers, where the two highways diverge. Turn left (southwest) onto CA 89, and go 5.1 miles to the signed Big Meadow trailhead on the left (north). Follow the short access road to the lower parking lot and the signed trailhead. GPS: N38 47.316' / W120 00.044'

The Hike

Mountain meadows witness the passage of the seasons in magical ways. In springtime and early summer, wildflowers erupt in pockets of red, purple, pink, orange, blue, white, and yellow, and the grasses vibrate with butterflies and bees harvesting nectar. By late summer and autumn, the flowers have faded, but the grasses have absorbed the warm hues of the summer sun, glistening gold and rattling in the breezes. Even in winter, blanketed in thick snow, a mountain meadow is meditative and impressive.

Big Meadow is perfect in all these incarnations.

To reach the meadow, begin in the lower trailhead parking area, just beyond the information sign. Pass a blue and white "Tahoe Rim Trail" sign almost immediately; the trail runs alongside CA 89 until it climbs to the edge of the asphalt and crosses the road.

The path steepens on the other side of the highway, ascending through a forest of mixed evergreens. Climb a log-and-granite staircase, which undoubtedly confounds mountain bikers navigating the route. Highway noise filters through the forest, but the rumbling of Big Meadow Creek helps mask the sound.

The trail flattens as the highway noises fade; the boulder-strewn woodland instead harbors birdsong and windsong. At the trail fork, go right (south), following the arrow that points to Meiss Meadow (aka Big Meadow); the left-hand trail leads to Scotts Lake.

Traverse a brief, final stretch of woodland, then the meadow opens. The path, worn into the turf, leads to a footbridge across the clear creek, then cuts a straight line through the grasses and wildflowers to the dense forest that

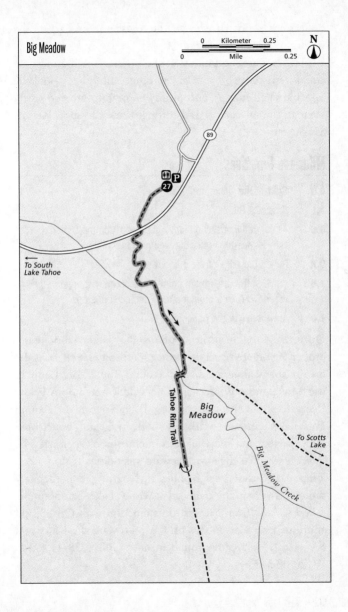

Big Meadow

0   Kilometer   0.25
0   Mile   0.25

N

89

27 P

← To South
Lake Tahoe

Tahoe Rim Trail

Big
Meadow

To Scotts
Lake

Big Meadow Creek

buffers the southern edge of the grassland and carpets the rolling mountains that cradle it.

The turnaround point is at the interface of the meadow and forest, though you can continue into the woodland. Sun-bleached stumps, once sturdy enough to provide restful seats and now cracked and rotting, mark the spot. Return as you came.

Miles and Directions

0.0 Start at the signed trailhead.

0.1 Cross CA 89.

0.6 At the trail intersection stay right (south) on the signed "Meiss Meadow" (aka Big Meadow) trail.

0.7 Reach the edge of the meadow.

1.0 Arrive at the turnaround point at the southwest edge of the meadow. Take a breather, then retrace your steps

2.0 Arrive back at the parking lot.

Option: Though it lies outside the Lake Tahoe basin proper, if you are traveling farther south on CA 89, consider hiking the Winnemucca and Round Top Lakes Loop in the Mokelumne Wilderness. The wildflower bloom below Winnemucca Lake is unsurpassed. The setting of Round Top Lake, below a dark sawtooth ridgeline punctuated with permanent snowfields, is picture-book perfect. The trail blends challenge with reward splendidly. Technically a lollipop, the route is 5.3 miles in length, and moderately difficult. To reach the trailhead at Woods Lake Campground, follow CA 89 from Meyers to its junction with CA 88, and continue over Carson Pass on CA 88 toward the Kirkwood ski resort to the campground turnoff. GPS: N38 41.493' / W120 00.573'

About the Author

Tracy Salcedo-Chourré has written more than twenty FalconGuides to destinations in California and Colorado, including *Hiking Lassen Volcanic National Park*, *Best Hikes Near Reno–Lake Tahoe*, *Best Hikes Near Sacramento*, *Exploring California's Missions and Presidios*, *Exploring Point Reyes National Seashore and the Golden Gate National Recreation Area*, *Best Rail Trails California*, and Best Easy Day Hikes guides to the San Francisco Bay Area, Lake Tahoe, Reno, Sacramento, Fresno, Boulder, Denver, and Aspen. She lives with her family in California's Wine Country. Visit laughingwaterink.com for more.